SECOND EDITION

TEACHING PHONICS TODAY

WORD STUDY STRATEGIES THROUGH THE GRADES

DOROTHY S. STRICKLAND

INTERNATIONAL Reading Association
800 BARKSDALE ROAD, PO BOX 8139
NEWARK, DE 19714-8139, USA
www.reading.org

Executive Editor, Books   Corinne M. Mooney
Developmental Editor   Charlene M. Nichols
Developmental Editor   Stacey L. Reid
Editorial Production Manager   Shannon T. Fortner
Design and Composition Manager   Anette Schuetz

Project Editors   Charlene Nichols and Christina M. Terranova

Cover   Design, Lise Holliker Dykes; Images, Thinkstock (illustrated letters) and Shutterstock (all others)

Photo Credits   Thinkstockphotos.com, pp. 9, 52, 83; Shutterstock Images LLC, pp. 14, 30, 40, 47.

The publisher would appreciate notification where errors occur so that they may be corrected in subsequent printings and/or editions.

Library of Congress Cataloging-in-Publication Data
Strickland, Dorothy S.
  Teaching phonics today : word study strategies through the grades / Dorothy S. Strickland. --
2nd ed.
     p. cm.
Includes bibliographical references and index.
ISBN 978-0-87207-827-7
1. Reading--Phonetic method. I. Title.
LB1573.3.S775 2011
372.46'5--dc22
                    2010046985

Suggested APA Reference
Strickland, D.S. (2011). *Teaching phonics today: Word study strategies through the grades* (second edition). Newark, DE: International Reading Association.

CONTENTS

ABOUT THE AUTHOR

 **Dorothy S. Strickland** is the Samuel DeWitt Proctor Professor of Education Emerita and Distinguished Research Fellow of the National Institute for Early Education Research at Rutgers, The State University of New Jersey, New Brunswick, USA. A former classroom teacher and learning disabilities specialist, she has authored and edited numerous publications concerning language development and reading. Recent publications include *Literacy Leadership in Early Childhood: The Essential Guide*; *Learning About Print in Preschool: Working With Letters, Words, and Beginning Links With Phonemic Awareness*; *Improving Reading Achievement Through Professional Development*; and *The Administration and Supervision of Reading Programs* (3rd edition).

A past president of both the International Reading Association (IRA) and the Reading Hall of Fame, Dorothy is the recipient of IRA's Outstanding Teacher Educator in Reading Award, the National Council of Teachers of English Award for Outstanding Educator in the English Language Arts, the Rewey Belle Inglis Award as Outstanding Woman in English Education, and the National-Louis University Ferguson Award for Outstanding Contributions to Early Childhood Education.

In 2008, she presented the annual Jeanne Chall Distinguished Address at Harvard University, and she is a frequent visiting professor and lecturer at other institutions. She has served on numerous boards and committees, including the National Early Literacy Panel and the panels that produced *Becoming a Nation of Readers: The Report of the Commission on Reading*, *Preventing Reading Difficulties in Young Children*, and *Reading for Understanding: Toward an R&D Program in Reading Comprehension*. She currently serves on a National Academy of Science panel on teacher preparation and the Validation Committee for the Common Core Standards. She was appointed by the governor to the New Jersey State Board of Education in 2008.

INTRODUCTION

Over the years, phonics has remained a controversial topic in the teaching of reading. Probably no other aspect of reading instruction has been more discussed, more hotly debated, and less understood. Classroom teachers and administrators are apt to be confronted by concerned members of the community who have questions about the inclusion of phonics in the beginning reading program. Given the amount of public interest in this topic, today's educators are likely to examine their beginning reading programs to determine whether they are consistent with current research on what is known about young children's early literacy development and about the strategies that support that development.

Today's educators seek to provide an evidence-based, balanced early literacy program that includes a strong foundation in word study strategies, including phonemic awareness and phonics. At the same time, they understand that the ultimate goal of early literacy instruction is to provide young children with a solid foundation toward becoming competent readers and writers, capable of comprehending texts presented to them in a variety of media and with the ability to apply what they read for a variety of purposes.

Although this book focuses on phonics, it is really about effective teaching. I believe that it is effective teaching that helps make phonics work for children as they learn to read and write. The organizational structure for this book reflects my major goal of illuminating the black hole of contention surrounding phonics with information that will help educators make wise instructional decisions.

Chapters 1 and 2 set forth the issues that focus on phonics and the controversy they inevitably invite. A research update, including the findings of recent reports, has been added to this edition. Chapters 3 and 4 explain the ways in which reading instruction, particularly the teaching of phonics, has evolved over the years. The national effort to adopt Common Core Standards for English Language Arts in the United States and the implications for all aspects of word study, including phonics, is addressed.

Chapters 5, 6, and 7 offer suggestions for helping children learn to use phonics as a key component of their overall reading development. New to this edition are strategies especially suited to struggling readers and writers beyond the primary grades. Chapter 5, for example, includes specific strategies for classroom intervention to prevent reading difficulties and to support children who are experiencing difficulty beyond the early grades. Suggestions for differentiating instruction and for working with English learners (ELs) are offered. These chapters also include suggestions for curriculum development, assessment, and articulating the phonics program to parents and the community at large. Each chapter ends with a feature called "Ideas to Think and Talk About." The topics and questions are designed for use by both preservice and inservice teachers.

It is my hope that this book will be a useful tool for those who wish to make sense of a topic that often divides faculties, parents, and community members. There is no doubt that there are legitimate differences among us about the role of phonics in our literacy programs, and these should be acknowledged and valued. There is also considerable common ground among us and an overwhelming similarity of purpose. I invite readers to use this book as a springboard for reflection and discussion and, ultimately, as a catalyst for making informed instructional decisions that help children become literate human beings.

—DSS

CHAPTER 1

Phonics: What Is It and Why Is It a Controversial Topic?

A discussion of phonics often evokes very different viewpoints, some even more disparate than those shown in Figure 1. Those who view phonics and its underpinnings as the most important and fundamental aspect of reading instruction and see it as the ultimate solution to illiteracy are on one side of the argument. Those for whom phonics is a worrisome topic, conjuring up images of children merely calling out the words and barking at print and ignoring meaning are on the other side.

A growing number of educators, parents, grandparents, and community members feel discomfort at either end of this continuum. This chapter provides a framework for those who seek to establish sound educational policy and instructional practice that values phonics as an important tool for understanding and using written language within a balanced, comprehensive program for reading and writing. Key research findings and the implications for curriculum and instruction are presented.

What Is Phonics?

Phonics refers to instruction in the sound–letter relationship used in reading and writing. It involves an understanding of the alphabetic

---

Figure 1. Opposing Voices

- "Today's teachers *don't* teach phonics. Our language is alphabetic. First, children should be taught the letters of the alphabet and the sounds that go with them and then they will be able to read."

- "Today's teachers *do* teach phonics. First, children need to learn that reading is supposed to make sense. Phonics should be taught, as needed, within the context of learning to read and write."

principle (i.e., there is a relation between spoken sounds and letters or combinations of letters) on which the English language is based and a knowledge of the sounds associated with a particular letter or combination of letters. For example, the letter *b* at the beginning of the word *back* and the combination of letters *ck* at the end of *back* each represent a single sound.

The ability to learn how sounds map to letters is related to *phonemic awareness*, or the understanding that speech itself is composed of a series of individual sounds (Goswami, 2001; Yopp, 1992). Before a child is capable of developing the concept of sound–symbol associations, he or she must understand that spoken words can be segmented. Children who are phonologically aware are able to discriminate between and manipulate sounds in words and syllables in speech. Figure 2 explains where phonics fits into the complex process of learning to read.

Phonologically aware children know when words rhyme or do not rhyme. They can indicate when a series of words begin or end with the same sound, such as *dog, dark,* and *dusty,* or *big, tag,* and *frog.* They also can break down or blend a series of sounds, such as /k/-/a/-/t/ in *cat.* Most important, these children can shift their attention from the content of speech to focus on the form of speech before they return to its meaning. Although the role of phonemic awareness in children's literacy development is not completely clear, researchers suggest that training in phonological awareness is both possible and advantageous for young

---

Figure 2. Where Phonics Fits in Literacy Learning and Teaching

- *Literacy* involves the ability to solve problems, think critically and creatively, and communicate effectively.
- *Literacy instruction* includes a planned program for the deliberate teaching of word identification skills and strategies that enable students to write effectively and to read with understanding.
- *Instruction for word identification* offers learners a range of organized and relatively systematic strategies to deal with unfamiliar words.
- *Phonics* is the ability to link written symbol and sound; it is included among the word identification strategies taught and learned in a comprehensive literacy program.
- In every subject area, students apply word identification strategies, including phonics, in varied situations with increasingly difficult materials.

children (Castiglioni-Spalten & Ehri, 2003). The development of phonemic awareness is generally stressed during kindergarten and early first grade. Some phonics instruction may begin in kindergarten, but it is generally emphasized during first and second grade.

Teachers and researchers are learning a great deal about how to help young children become aware that spoken language can be taken apart and how this understanding supports and eases the learning of phonics. However, questions remain about how much phonemic awareness is necessary to develop ability in decoding and how much is acquired in a reciprocal, mutually supportive relationship with learning to read (Castles & Coltheart, 2004; Weaver, 1998). Kindergarten teachers have always built on children's affinity for alliteration and rhyme in nursery rhymes and children's songs. Young children also have the benefit of their participation in the language of popular culture, which is filled with terms such as *hip hop* or *backpack* that foster sensitivity to the sounds of language.

Structural analysis is a term that often is confused with phonics. It involves a knowledge of the structural changes that differentiate words having common roots: inflectional endings (i.e., *-s, -ed, -ing*), prefixes and suffixes (e.g., *pre-, un-, -tion, -ment*), and root words (e.g., *prepaid, unpaid, repaid*). Instruction in structural analysis usually begins in first grade, where teachers help children learn about rules such as adding *s* to form plurals and the formation of compound words such as *raincoat* and *snowman*. It continues through children's schooling as they encounter increasingly complex language structures.

Over the years, phonics has come to mean much more than the definition presented earlier. In the minds of many educators, phonics and beginning reading are synonymous. Indeed, most teachers of beginning reading include a broad array of skills and activities under the heading of phonics. The teaching of letter recognition, rhyming words, and spelling patterns generally is considered to be part of phonics instruction. Phonics often is referred to as a method or program of teaching reading, but it is really a set of instructional strategies that helps learners connect sounds with written symbols. Nevertheless, any instruction that places an emphasis on the teaching of sound–letter correspondences frequently is termed a *phonics method.*

Concern and Controversy

Historically, those who have denounced poor reading achievement in the United States have turned to phonics as a solution. A brief look at some of the historical perspectives and influences on reading instruction help explain the circumstances and conditions that have brought us to where we are today.

During the colonial period in the United States, an alphabet spelling system dominated the teaching of reading. Instruction was directed toward a single purpose, the reading of religious books by a limited few who were actually taught to read. In the early 1800s, Horace Mann introduced the whole-word method of teaching reading. He stressed memorizing entire words before analyzing letters and letter patterns, and he focused on silent reading and reading for comprehension. The *McGuffey Eclectic Readers* also were introduced around this time. These readers made use of the controlled repetition of words and an organizational scheme in which sentence length and vocabulary were controlled to match the developmental level of students.

During the latter half of the 19th century, a phonetics method was introduced in which children were taught individual sound–letter relations and how to blend them to read words. Teachers became dissatisfied with this method because too much attention was placed on word analysis and too little attention was given to comprehension. This approach was temporarily abandoned around 1910 and replaced with the "look-and-say" method. This method also proved unsatisfactory to many teachers. Children were expected to learn every word as a sight word, making progress slow and laborious.

About 1920, the silent reading method emerged as the official approach in many schools. This method urged the total abandonment of all oral methods of instruction and assessment. About this time, widespread administration of standardized tests called the public's attention to the vast individual differences in reading achievement among children. It also inspired teachers to try new instructional methods to better accommodate individual differences. Research during this era gave rise to an extremely popular approach that followed—the basal reading program—which was launched throughout the United States in the early 1930s.

The "Dick and Jane" readers (and others like them), as basal programs would come to be known, became the staple of reading instruction methodology in the United States for several decades. Basal reading programs predominated over other methods until the early 1960s, when teachers became dissatisfied with them as the only form of reading instruction and again returned to phonics. Educators wanted more organized skill-development programs and more attention to reading in the content subjects. Specialized phonics programs were introduced into many schools to augment the basal or core literacy program.

The on-again off-again fascination with phonics has been inspired to some extent by media reports of illiteracy among the military, of international events, and of standardized test results. For example, during both World War I and World War II, the U.S. military charged that too many members could not read well enough to follow military instructions. Such reports received considerable attention in the news and caused understandable concern among the public. During the 1950s and 1960s, media reports of *Sputnik*, the Cold War, and the threat of atomic weapons also made literacy a national imperative in the United States. Interest in reading instruction soared during this period, with laymen and the media criticizing the schools' methods and calling for decisive action. One of the most vocal proponents of phonics was Rudolph Flesch (1955), whose book *Why Johnny Can't Read: And What You Can Do About It* hailed phonics as the cure for what he perceived as widespread and growing illiteracy.

The Research Base

Concern for the disparities in reading achievement among children in the United States has persisted through the years. Although many children do not learn to read as well as expected, others reach high levels of proficiency. During the 1960s, numerous research studies were conducted to determine why some children, particularly poor and minority children, were not succeeding. Educational researchers engaged in numerous studies comparing various approaches to reading instruction in controlled studies designed to demonstrate superiority. The most famous of these, the Cooperative Research Program in First-Grade Reading Instruction (commonly referred to as the "First-Grade Studies"), was designed to compare a traditional basal program with various other approaches (Bond & Dykstra, 1967/1997).

Unfortunately, no strong conclusion could be drawn from these studies. No one approach was so distinctly better in all situations and respects than the others that it could be considered the best method to be used exclusively. The publication of *Learning to Read: The Great Debate* (Chall, 1967) brought considerable attention to the phonics debate. Chall examined the existing research literature for evidence related to questions regarding the best way to approach beginning reading. She concluded that "a code emphasis tends to produce better overall reading achievement by the beginning of fourth grade than a meaning emphasis" (p. 137).

Chall's conclusions regarding beginning instruction were challenged by many (e.g., Rutherford, 1968), raising questions about the validity of the research studies on which she based her conclusions and the arbitrary nature of her classification system into code- and meaning-emphasis categories. Although Chall did not suggest that her findings be used to endorse systematic phonics approaches, her work has been highly influential in support of those who endorse a heavy emphasis on phonics in beginning reading.

More recent research reports have had considerable influence on the teaching of reading. These reports confirmed the importance of phonics found by previous studies without endorsing any specific teaching method. The report of the National Reading Panel, *Teaching Children to Read: An Evidence-Based Assessment of the Scientific Research Literature on Reading and Its Implications for Reading Instruction* (National Institute of Child Health and Human Development [NICHD], 2000), is arguably one of the most influential studies on reading. This report also confirmed many of the studies that preceded it. Alphabetics (i.e., phonemic awareness instruction and phonics) is once again mentioned as a key foundational aspect of learning to read. Attention to fluency, comprehension, and vocabulary instruction was also stressed. This report confirmed the need for meaningful practice. Comprehension is described as the construction of meaning through the application of intentional, problem-solving processes while interacting with written text. Comprehension involves all the elements of the reading process acting together: phonemic awareness, phonics, fluency, vocabulary, and text comprehension.

Developing Early Literacy: Report of the National Early Literacy Panel (National Institute for Literacy, 2008) was designed to provide a synthesis of research on the development of early literacy in young

Kindergarten children identify letters as part of an alphabet game.

children, prior to first grade. The researchers sought to determine the skills and abilities young children require to help them grow into successful readers and writers. Key predictive skills and abilities found to be related to success in reading were alphabet knowledge, phonological/phonemic awareness, knowledge about print, and oral language development. Effective instructional strategies included shared reading that encouraged reader–child interaction and one-on-one and small-group instructional interventions. Successful parent and home programs were found to foster children's oral language and cognitive development. Strickland and Shanahan (2004) provided a discussion of the findings and their implications for instruction at the prekindergarten and early kindergarten levels.

The Place of Phonics in the Reading Curriculum

Various changes in methodology were initiated during the 1960s and early 1970s in an attempt to solve the reading problem in the United States. Programmed materials were developed to provide better classroom management techniques. The language experience approach, which advocated the use of children's own dictated language as an introduction to reading, was promoted as an effective teaching method. Linguistics began to influence the structure of some basal readers. Linguists promoted the teaching of reading through patterned word units such as *Pat sat on a mat.* Materials dealing with multiethnic, urban environments were introduced to answer the criticism that basals tended to reflect the values and mores of white, middle-class United States. Teachers were encouraged to address the needs of diverse readers by personalizing programs to suit individual needs.

Researchers, educators, and publishers of reading materials continued to address an ever-expanding set of new and complex challenges, as schools faced an increasingly diverse population and a society in which the schools were called on to take on more and more responsibility. Reports showing criticism of public schools, such as *A Nation at Risk: The Imperative for Educational Reform* (National Commission on Excellence in Education, 1983), reinforced negative public opinion about the schools. Even when statements included in the reports—such as the assertion of a decline in overall student achievement in the United States—proved to be contradictory or incorrect, disparagement of the schools and the teaching of reading remained constant (Berliner & Biddle, 1995; Kibby, 1993).

During the 1990s, reading systems published by a few major publishing companies continued to dominate the materials and methodology used to teach reading. Although these expanded basals differed in some ways, virtually all had changed in similar ways. One of the most noticeable changes was the inclusion of authentic literature (such as the text of trade books) in the students' anthologies.

Prior to this time, most of the material at the primary-grade levels and some at the elementary levels was written specifically for inclusion in basal reading systems. This was done to maintain control of vocabulary, sentence length, and other factors believed to contribute to readability. The inclusion of authentic literature with relatively few changes from the original text was a major departure. Another important difference was the expansion of reading programs to include instruction in all the language arts, particularly writing and spelling. Many reading programs were now called "integrated language arts programs" or "total literacy programs," indicating that a separate program for writing and oral language would no longer be needed.

The move toward integrated approaches to the teaching of the English language arts (i.e., listening, speaking, reading, writing) in the elementary schools was inspired by several new directions in the research and thinking of many influential educators in the United States and other English-speaking countries. Perhaps more than ever before, the work of research in the field of reading was informed by cognitive and developmental psychology, sociology, linguistics, literary theory, and a growing interest in research on writing in the elementary school. The ideas generated from this cross-fertilization and collaboration of researchers from various disciplines helped to establish a rationale for treating language as a meaningful whole rather than as a set of discrete subskills.

Integrated, literature-based approaches to reading instruction in which phonics is taught in conjunction with other word identification strategies were among the practical applications. The tension between these newer approaches—though widely varied in application—and approaches based on a phonics emphasis or a particular approach to the teaching of phonics continues to be felt today.

Sometimes the support of phonics is combined with demands for a greater emphasis on spelling and grammar and a return to instructional practices of the past. Discussions surrounding these issues often come to represent much more than the concerns associated with reading instruction. In some districts, the phonics controversy reveals deep philosophical differences about teaching and learning and leads to power struggles over educational policy. Despite the potential for the phonics debate to polarize educational communities, most educators and parents try to avoid instructional pendulum swings that confuse rather than clarify issues. Instead, they choose to concentrate their efforts on providing effective literacy programs that are informed by the best research and practice available.

IDEAS TO THINK AND TALK ABOUT

1. What comes to mind when you think of the term *phonics*?
2. What can you remember about phonics in your own early literacy experiences?
3. How do you think things are the same or different today?

CHAPTER 2

How Readers and Writers Use Phonics

This chapter addresses the role of phonics in the broad, complex frame of language and literacy development. Long before they attempt to read and write, young children make use of *semantic cues* (i.e., meaning) and *syntactic cues* (i.e., grammar) to create meaning. If you said to a 3-year-old, "I'm thinking of something I'd like for dinner, and it's _____ ," the child might offer the following: hot dogs, hamburgers, ice cream. The word(s) the child gives undoubtedly would be something he or she had experienced or would like to experience for dinner and would fit syntactically, structurally, or grammatically in the slot provided. In other words, the child would respond to the meaning or semantic cues by only offering words that represent food. Similarly, a response such as *jumped* is highly unlikely. Even for a very young child, the sentence "I'm thinking of something I'd like for dinner, and it's jumped," would be unacceptable. As speakers of English, children will offer words they think sound right in the open slot in the sentence. Thus, children offer grammatically appropriate nouns as they demonstrate sensitivity to the syntax of their language.

By the time children begin to read and write, they already have some knowledge of how oral language works. However, this does not alter their need for knowledge of sound–letter relationships; it simply means that they already have some important knowledge on which word identification strategies may be based.

Common Word Identification Strategies for Reading

Reading is a highly complex process in which many sources of information are used to understand written texts, and young children bring a variety of information to the task of learning to read. By the time they enter first grade, most children have attained a high degree of control over their language. Even youngsters whose first language or dialect is not standard English have developed language systems that can be used as the basis for reading instruction. They not only have a high degree of control over the sounds of their language, but they also possess large vocabularies, including words that name the content of their world and represent complex sets of meanings, and they have strategies for constructing a variety of simple and complex sentences. Their knowledge of oral language may be the most important thing that children bring to the task of learning to read. It serves as a foundation for learning the many conventions and features of printed language, such as directionality, spacing, and punctuation that are strange and new to beginning readers.

To identify words and comprehend written messages, readers use their knowledge of language and their personal experience as well as the print and pictures on the page. They employ strategies that make use of various code cues or prompts, which signal a particular tactic or combination of tactics for use in *decoding* (i.e., reading) or *encoding* (i.e., writing) messages in text. Decoding refers to the entire set of strategies readers use to "unlock the code," as shown in Figure 3. To most teachers and parents, however, decoding simply refers to the use of phonics to determine the pronunciation of words.

Some word identification strategies develop long before children are given formal instruction in reading. Emergent readers and writers use environmental cues from their everyday surroundings to signal what a word or group of words might be. Logos for fast-food restaurants are recognized by children as young as 2 years old. Many young children learn to read the word *STOP* on the traffic sign and, if they live in a high-rise apartment,

---

Figure 3. Strategies for Word Identification: Decoding

Early Strategies		Ongoing Strategies
Make use of...	>>>	Make use of...
Environmental cues	give	Graphophonic (phonics) cues
Picture cues	way	Semantic (meaning) cues
Configuration (word form) cues	to	Syntactic (grammar/sentence structure) cues
	>>>	Structural analysis (root words, word parts)
		Background knowledge

A young student reads his book by using phonics together with picture cues.

they are likely to learn the words *up* and *down* from using the elevator. Whether children respond to the entire logo or to graphic cues on a particular word or letter, they often look quite phenomenal as they identify breakfast cereal brands and fast-food restaurants.

Picture cues offer another aid to word identification during children's very early years. Illustrations on a book or household product signal the written message to the reader. Later, when children begin formal instruction, they may be instructed to use illustrations only in conjunction with more relevant word identification strategies to decode an unknown word. Obviously, as children are confronted with an increasing amount of text and fewer illustrations, reliance on illustrations as a sole strategy for word identification loses its value.

Configuration cues also may be helpful to emerging readers and writers. Unusual visual patterns or unique letter forms, such as double letters in *little* or the letter *y* at the end of *baby*, may be sufficiently striking to cause young readers to remember them although their reading vocabularies still are very limited. However, like picture cues, configuration cues have short-term use.

As children move beyond the emergent stages of literacy and begin to approach reading and writing in a more formal way, knowledge of *graphophonic cues* (i.e., letters, letter clusters, corresponding sounds) becomes essential. Thus, the use of phonics along with the use of context or semantic cues, syntactic cues, and broader textual meanings become important interrelated strategies for word identification. Because of their interrelated nature, graphophonics, semantics, and syntax are commonly referred to as the *three cueing systems* of reading.

A reader's *background knowledge* plays a major role in the use of context clues. Even the very best decoder may miss the message if the content is outside his or her experience. For example, a child who gets stuck on the word *davenport* in the sentence, *Mary sat down to rest on the davenport*, may have no difficulty pronouncing all the words, but may remain unaware that Mary was resting on a couch.

Finally, *structural analysis cues* involve the use of structural elements in words to identify them. As mentioned earlier, this includes inflectional endings (e.g., *-s, -ed, -ing*), prefixes and suffixes (e.g., *pre-, un-, -tion*), root words (e.g., *playful, playmate*), and compound words (e.g., *raincoat, airplane*). Regardless of the word recognition strategies used, readers must verify their identification of an unfamiliar word by cross-checking to determine whether it fits the context. If the word does not make sense, readers must try another strategy. For example, in the sentence, *Without his gloves, John's hands were cold*, a young reader might use semantic cues for cross-checking purposes in order to identify the word *gloves*, which does not fit the vowel generalization rule for words of this type. One consequence of cross-checking is metacognitive, or conscious, awareness of the success of word identification (Fox, 1996).

The use of *word families, phonograms*, or *spelling patterns* (e.g., *at* in *bat, cat, fat*) has been validated in several research efforts as an important strategy for identifying words (Moustafa, 1995; Treiman, 1985). Both children and adults find it more effective to divide syllables into their *onsets* (i.e., all letters before the vowel) and *rimes* (i.e., the vowel and what follows) than into any other units. Thus, the word *bat* is more easily divided into *b-at* than into *ba-t* or *b-a-t*. This research has led some to suggest that young children are likely to rely on their knowledge of onsets and rimes rather than rely on their knowledge of individual letters and related sounds to pronounce unfamiliar words.

According to Moustafa (1997), children move from whole to parts: (1) They learn whole print words in which they remember the letters and the pronunciation together; (2) as they learn to recognize more and more print words, they encounter some with like letters or letter strings representing like onsets or rimes (e.g., *smiles* and *small*); (3) they begin to learn the pronunciation of the parts of those words (e.g., *sm* is pronounced /sm/, *iles* is pronounced /ilz/, *all* is pronounced /al/) and begin to figure out the parts of the words; and (4) finally, as they encounter unfamiliar print words (such as *smart* and *tiles*), they make analogies at the onset–rime level. Children's use of onset–rime analogy provides new understandings about how young children learn to read the English language, which is both an onset–rime and an alphabetic system. Emphasis on this strategy has shown particular promise for students who have failed in their initial attempts to learn to read (Ehri & Roberts, 2006).

Phonics and Spelling

Learning to spell is highly related to learning to read (Ehri & Roberts, 2006). Writers use phonics to aid them in spelling the words they use to communicate ideas. Although most experienced writers spell with ease and accuracy, young writers find correct spelling to be one of the most challenging aspects of writing. Young writers have been known to change their text in order to accommodate their spelling needs. A teacher shared a story about a child who asked for help in spelling the word *piano*. He was writing the sentence, *My mother loves to play piano.* The teacher encouraged him to try spelling it on his own, only to discover later that he had revised the sentence to read, *My mother loves to play ball.* Effective teachers are aware of the need to provide an environment in which students feel comfortable enough to take risks in applying what they know. Children are fortunate when they have frequent opportunities for self-expression through writing such as the example shown in Figure 4. These are students who grow in their awareness of phonics rules and gain greater control over them.

For many years, it was thought that learning to read was a prerequisite to learning to write and spell. In fact, attention to young children's writing is relatively recent. However, observations of preschool children in settings where they are encouraged to write independently reveal that

Figure 4. Picture and Example of a Kindergarten Child's Invented Spelling

SMP

Child: I am swimming in the pool.

Kindergarten (May)

many begin to develop strategies for spelling based on their knowledge of the phonological system and their knowledge of letter names (Read, 1971, 1975). Figure 4 shows how a kindergarten child makes use of his knowledge of letters and sounds to label his picture. As spellers become more experienced with written language, they learn to combine their knowledge of sound–letter relationships, their visual memories of how words look, and their morphemic knowledge (i.e., their knowledge of words and word parts) to spell the words they need. A *morpheme* is the smallest unit of meaning in written language. Children build their knowledge of morphemes through abundant exposure to print and through direct instruction. For example, the *ed* in *wanted* and *ma* in *grandma* both are morphemic units. The chart shown in Figure 5 helps to explain how even very young writers use these spelling strategies.

Children's early independent spelling is sometimes referred to as *invented spelling, temporary spelling, constructive spelling, developmental spelling,* or *phonics-based spelling.* At first, these early spellings are the result of a child's natural encounters with print. Later, spellings become more and more conventional as children are increasingly exposed to written language and as they apply what they learn through both informal and formal instruction. There appears to be no rigid sequence of development that all children follow as they learn to spell. In Figure 6, Powell and Hornsby (1993) describe three categories of development that show what might be expected when children apply what they know about written language and phonics as they spell. Obviously the writing of any individual child may include a variety of spelling behaviors across the three categories.

Figure 5. Common Spelling Strategies Used by Beginning Writers

Sound–letter knowledge: *I think I know which letters go with the sounds I hear.*
Examples: (1) I think *ball* starts like /b/ in Billy's name. The last part rhymes with *call.*
          (2) From the way *crash* sounds, I think it begins with *cr.*
             I hear /a/ in the middle, so there must be an *a,* and it sounds like it ends with *sh.*

Visual memory: *I remember how that word looks.*
Examples: (1) I remember the word *puppy* has two *p*'s in the middle of the word, not just one.
          (2) The word *friend* does not fit the rules, but I remember how it looks in the middle.

Knowledge of words and word parts: *I can use something I know about other words or parts of words to help me spell this one.*
Examples: (1) *Rice* is almost like *mice.* I simply need to change the beginning.
          (2) I can change the end of *looks* to spell *looking.*

Figure 6. Three Categories of Development

EMERGENT SPELLERS

Emergent spellers understand the function of print. They begin to use print to communicate meaning, but they don't have sufficient graphophonic knowledge to communicate a message through writing alone because they use predominantly temporary spellings.

Observations:

- uses letter—like symbols
- no indication that child has:
  1. letter knowledge
  2. letter/sound correspondences
  3. sense of wordness
- has idea that print carries message

Three Billy Goats Gruff, but there are six.

Observations:

- uses both initial and final sounds of words
- several conventional spellings
- capitalized *I* in second use
- uses dash to indicate letters missing
- uses some vowels
- word segmentation not evident

I was at the school today and I went to the gym today.

(continued)

Figure 6. Three Categories of Development (continued)

NOVICE SPELLERS

Novice spellers have enough graphophonic knowledge to communicate meaning to others, but they use temporary spelling when writing unknown words and sometimes even when writing words they have frequently written before. They predominantly use phonic strategies for spelling.

Observations:

- word segmentation
- may need assistance with placement on page
- uses vowels consistently
- uncertainty of some spelling patterns (such as *sh*)
- uses primarily uppercase letters

Observations:

- most sounds represented with reasonable letter/sounds
- many conventionally spelled words
- word segmentation used
- spacing on page may need attention
- mixes lowercase and uppercase
- vowels used consistently in each syllable

(continued)

Figure 6. Three Categories of Development (continued)

INDEPENDENT SPELLERS

Independent spellers use conventional spelling for most words
frequently written, and they have developed efficient strategies for
spelling unknown words. They have also developed proofreading
strategies.

Observations:

- mostly correct spelling
- knows hyphenated vowels
  and contractions
- mixes lower- and
  uppercase letters
- uses letter format
- needs attention on
  punctuation and capitals

Dear Scott

I hope you get to Be A
Teacher THIS is my First
Time To Be A pen-Pal Aid IS
FUn Being youer peh-Pal. if
you AreMy Teacher Thenyou'Be
AS good AS Any. Other Teacher.
I hAve to puppies do you have
Any PeTs

from you'en pen-PAl

DAVid

Observations:

- mostly correct spelling
- knows hyphenated words,
  compound words
- spells plural forms
- proofreading skills not
  apparent

Dress-Up

I like to dress up with Jennifer.
We put onfancy dresses and
gloves and very pretty Purses.
We put on high hill shoes. And
We put on Make up. And we
like to play house with the
dresses. Some day I with that
I can wear every thing in
Public, but I dought it.

The End

From *Learning Phonics and Spelling* by Debbie Powell and David Hornsby. Copyright © 1993 Debbie Powell
and David Hornsby. Reprinted by permission of Scholastic Inc.

Assessing Progress

Documenting children's development of phonics is an important part of early literacy education. Assessment that reveals how children make use of phonics in authentic situations is preferable over those that simply require children to match sounds (i.e., phonemes) and symbols (i.e., letters) in isolation. For example, when shown the letter *t*, a child may respond with the sound it usually represents and still not be able to apply that information in their reading and writing. Encouraging and documenting children's developing use of decoding strategies, such as those described in this chapter, is an important means of tracking growth. It also provides the documentation required for appropriate intervention referrals.

Perhaps the most revealing evidence of children's acquisition and use of phonics is reflected in their authentic writing. Figure 7, Writing/Phonics and Spelling Assessment Record (Pre K–3), offers a formative assessment strategy for collecting and recording student progress in applying phonics in their writing. Student writing samples are collected periodically and kept in a portfolio. They are used to make instructional decisions and for conferences with the child, other relevant professionals, and parents.

Knowing the limitations of achievement testing, particularly for very young children, and using the categories from *Learning Phonics and Spelling* (Powell & Hornsby, 1993) such as those presented, can help teachers track children's progress over time and avoid the use of standardized measures that assess sound–symbol relationships in isolation of real text. Over time, as teachers look at the progress of individual children and across the group, this kind of assessment yields useful information of three types:

1. The child in relation to himself or herself—How well is a child doing today compared with a previous time?
2. The child in relation to the group—How well is a child doing in relation to others in the group?
3. The group as a whole—Are there areas where many children are having difficulty? What changes in the curriculum may be necessary?

Perhaps most important, this kind of assessment requires teachers to thoughtfully examine the results of classroom instruction and make

Figure 7. Writing/Phonics and Spelling Assessment Record (Pre K–3)

CHILD'S NAME _____ GRADE _____

Developmental Categories

• *Emergent spellers* understand the functions of print. They begin to use print to communicate meaning, but they do not have sufficient graphophonic knowledge to communicate a message through writing alone because they use predominantly temporary spellings.

• *Novice spellers* have enough graphophonic knowledge to communicate meaning to others, but they use temporary spelling when writing unknown words and sometimes even when writing words they have frequently written before. They predominantly use phonic strategies for spelling.

• *Independent spellers** use conventional spelling for most words frequently written, and they have developed efficient strategies for spelling unknown words. They have also developed proofreading strategies.

Date	Developmental Category	Observations and Notes

*based on Powell and Hornsby (1993)

informed decisions that truly reflect children's acquisition and application of knowledge about reading.

Making the Best Use of Phonics

Good readers automatically recognize words that they encounter regularly. They do this by using their knowledge of letters and sounds, as well as by selecting and combining a variety of other strategies for word identification. Good writers use phonics in much the same way. Because our writing system is alphabetic, the use of sound–letter knowledge is a logical strategy for gaining independence as a reader and writer. It always must be kept in mind, however, that phonics does not stand alone. It is used during reading and spelling, and its use is informed by reading and spelling. In other words, readers use what they learn about phonics during writing, and writers are helped to spell by what they have learned about phonics through reading. Phonics is influenced greatly by the language context in which it is applied. It is reasonable to assume that young readers and writers who have a range of word identification strategies will make the best use of phonics. Figure 8 offers some guidelines, based on research and experience, for use in helping children learn phonics.

Phonics and its role in learning to read is a topic that is highly controversial and often is misunderstood. It is frequently used as a catch-all term to stand for a return to the "basics." This is particularly true when students' achievement in reading does not meet expectations. Many

---

Figure 8. Suggested Guidelines for Learning and Teaching Phonics

- Teaching phonics is *not* synonymous with teaching reading.
- Reading and spelling require much more than phonics.
- Phonics is a means to an end, not the end itself.
- Phonics is one of several enablers or cueing systems that help us read.
- Phonics is one of several strategies for spelling.
- Memorizing phonics rules does not ensure application of those rules.
- Learners need to see the relevance of phonics for themselves in their own reading and writing.
- Teaching students to use phonics is different from teaching them *about* phonics.
- The best context for learning and applying phonics is actual reading and writing.

---

educators, whether they are new or experienced, are attempting to become better informed about phonics and its role in providing a balanced and effective reading program.

IDEAS TO THINK AND TALK ABOUT

1. Use the information in Figure 6 to reflect on the differences in emergent, novice, and independent spellers.
2. Discuss the many ways that phonics is used by readers and spellers in conjunction with other word study and writing strategies.

CHAPTER 3

Trends in Literacy Instruction and Their Influence on the Teaching of Phonics

Ｎew insights into learning and teaching have produced numerous changes in the ways reading and writing are taught. Among the most noticeable trends are (a) greater emphasis on writing and its relation to reading; (b) increased attention to the integration of all the language arts; (c) greater use of a variety of materials, including trade books and library books; and (d) greater reliance on informal classroom assessment. This chapter offers a brief description of each trend and how it affects literacy instruction in general and phonics in particular.

Greater Emphasis on Writing and Its Relation to Reading

Until the 1980s, very little attention was given to writing instruction during the elementary years (Teale & Yokota, 2000). Handwriting always has been stressed in elementary classrooms, but attention to the composition of stories and expository texts was quite limited. Things have changed. Even the youngest students now are given opportunities to communicate through written language on a daily basis. Teachers emphasize the processes involved, including selecting and framing a topic, creating and revising drafts, and editing, so that what is written may be shared with others. Teachers of young children are aware that children's attempts to write encourage their interest in and need for the alphabetic code. Thus, much of today's phonics instruction takes place during writing. Phonics is linked to reading as a tool for word identification and to writing as a tool for spelling.

Teachers No Longer Treat Copying as Writing

Until the 1980s, much of what a child wrote in first grade consisted of copying from a chalkboard. The material may have been composed by the class, but more often it was composed by the teacher and then read in unison by the class before it was copied. Teachers emphasized handwriting and neatness (see Figure 9). It was generally assumed that children needed a fairly substantial spelling vocabulary and some word recognition skills before they could be expected to compose their own material. Even then, a heavy emphasis was placed on mechanical correctness of written language, and little attention was given to the content or the act of composing. Because children's writing tended to be restricted only to what they could write without errors, it consisted primarily of short, highly prosaic sentences much like those they normally copied from the board.

What does the child whose work is in Figure 9 know about written language? Josh knows how to copy successfully from the board and forms

Figure 9. Example of a First-Grade Student's Copying/Handwriting Exercise

Today is Friday.
It is raining.
Monday is the birthday of
Martin Luther King.
          Josh
        Grade 1

letters correctly and neatly. He may have an understanding of the concept of space between words in written language. It cannot be assumed that Josh is able to read back what he copied.

Teachers Now Encourage Beginning Readers and Writers to Make Personal Attempts at Writing

From the earliest grades, today's students are encouraged to communicate through writing (see Figure 10). Because they may have had the benefit of only a minimum amount of instruction in reading and writing, they can be expected to make mistakes. The mistakes they make usually are quite inventive and informing because children use their knowledge about written language to give as close an approximation to conventional spelling as they can. Keep in mind that *these attempts do not replace deliberate instruction in phonics.* However, opportunities to write are an important part of this instruction. Through a series of mutually supportive opportunities for both direct and indirect instruction, children use phonics to develop skill in spelling and competence in their ability to communicate effectively through writing.

What does the child whose work is in Figure 10 know about written language? First and most important, this child knows how to express her

---

Figure 10. Example of a First-Grade Student Communicating Through Writing

Responding to literature about Martin Luther King, Jr., which was read aloud by her teacher and discussed by her first-grade class, Tiesha wrote:

I HAVE A DREAM THAT SOMEDAY . . .

Piepl wood stop fteing
(People would stop fighting)

becoa's ther the sam
(because they're the same)

ther jaut's derfit colers.
(they're just different colors.)

Tiesha M.
Grade 1

---

personal ideas through her own independent writing. Tiesha knows that in written language there are spaces between words. She is beginning to understand the use of capital letters at the beginning of a sentence and a period at the end. She has command of the sound–letter relationship of *p* in both the initial and medial position of the word *people*. Other consonant sound–letter relationships she uses correctly are represented by *b* in *because*; *th* in *they're*; *s* in *same*; *d*, *f*, and *t* in *different*; and *c* in *color*. She has correctly spelled the word *wood*, but needs help with the homophone (*wood/would*). She correctly uses the inflectional ending *ing*. The lack of an *e* at the end of the word *same* indicates that Tiesha may be ready for attention to the vowel generalization regarding the *e* marker at the end of short words of this type (i.e., first vowel is long; *e* is silent). She uses conventional spellings for the words *stop* and *the*. It is likely that Tiesha can read what she wrote.

Increased Attention to the Integration of All the Language Arts

Research into the nature of language learning has caused many to change their view of language as a complex system in which the parts—listening, speaking, reading, and writing with each other and across the curriculum—are both integrated and interdependent. When an individual component is isolated from the written language system, it no longer functions as it does within real reading and writing. The interdependent nature of the elements of language becomes highly evident when phonics rules are applied too rigidly. For example, the letter string *r-e-a-d* is pronounced very differently depending on the context in which it is presented: "Yesterday, I *read* the entire sports page; I hope I'll have time to *read* today's as well." The rule that applies here states that when two vowels are side by side, the long sound of the first one is heard and the second usually is silent.

Clymer (1996) reports on the utility of 45 phonic generalizations. Many elementary teachers were shocked to learn that this widely taught generalization about two vowels side by side was listed as having 309 conforming words (such as *bead*) and 377 exceptions (such as *chief*), so it was useful less than 50% of the time. As one teacher put it, "Mr. Clymer, for years I've been teaching 'When two vowels go walking, the first one

A teacher assists an elementary-grade student with word study strategies.

does the talking.' You're ruining the romance in the teaching of reading!" (p. 187).

The fact that most of the phonic generalizations taught in elementary school are not valid much of the time does not suggest that they should never be taught. In addition to the rule cited earlier, the following vowel generalizations generally are considered useful for primary-grade students: (a) When there are two vowels in a word, one of which is final *e*, the first vowel is long and the final *e* is silent (63%); and (b) When a vowel is in the middle of a one-syllable word, the vowel usually is short (62%). Teachers should avoid teaching these generalizations as rules to be memorized; rather, they should be taught as examples of language patterns that may be put to strategic use for reading and spelling.

Most important, teachers should be aware of studies such as Clymer's (1996) in order to make instructional decisions based on what will be most useful to students and to anticipate potential confusion and difficulty. This research speaks to the need to provide students with multiple word recognition strategies. Overreliance on any one strategy, including phonics, actually may hinder young readers and writers. They need to learn early that the pronunciation and meaning of words are influenced not only by the way they look, but by the language context in which they are found.

Teachers Balance Knowledge and Application of Phonics by Emphasizing Its Use Across the Language Arts

During the 1930s, the organizational pattern in which children were placed in long-term groups according to ability emerged as the preferred approach to addressing individual differences in reading ability. Listening, speaking, and writing were addressed separately and were given less instructional emphasis than reading. Spelling was taught as a discrete subject totally unrelated to writing. When spelling was considered within the context of writing, it was largely to note errors. Little was done to help students self-edit for spelling or make note of the kinds of spelling errors made during writing.

Even phonics can be taught as a distinct activity separate from the time spent reading books in small groups. Rather than be introduced to sound–letter relationships as textual patterns found in familiar literature, most teachers taught these relations in a particular sequence and in isolation from real text. For this type of instruction, teachers made use of phonics kits or workbook exercises and employed a whole-group instructional format. Although many children successfully applied what was learned, many others failed to make the connection between phonics and its application to reading or spelling.

With so much emphasis given to phonics as an isolated subject, some students tended to rely almost exclusively on phonics, making little use of other word recognition strategies that might, if used in combination with phonics, help them to make better use of what they knew about sound–letter relationships. Students were subjected to large amounts of phonics whether they needed it or not. Children who already were reading were likely to get the same amount of phonics instruction as those who arrived at school with relatively few prior experiences at home with books and print. Children with limited exposure to print might receive heavy phonics instruction before they had sufficient understandings about print to facilitate its application.

Language Arts Instruction Is Organized Around Large Blocks of Time in Which Oral Language and Written Language Are Taught in an Integrated Way

A growing number of teachers have devoted a block of their teaching day to emphasize language arts. In the primary grades, this might be as much as 90 minutes or more. A large part of this time is devoted to reading instruction. However, strong connections are made with writing and oral language by using whole texts to identify aspects of language for in-depth study. Specific strategies addressed include those that make use of phonemic awareness, phonics, or structural analysis along with aspects of reading comprehension and the writing process. Phonics is linked to both reading and spelling. Its knowledge provides the basis of one of several word recognition strategies; for example, the use of semantics or meaning can confirm phonics when applied to an unknown word.

Children are encouraged to do a great deal of independent reading and writing in which they are urged to apply what they have learned. Children are held accountable for what they are taught. They are encouraged to use prior knowledge to make attempts to figure out what they may not know. Gradually, as they gain experience and receive more instruction, their spelling becomes more conventional and their reading more fluent.

Figure 11 depicts how a teacher might conceptualize a lesson or series of lessons that attempt to help students look at the parts of language in the context of the whole. Children are exposed to examples of the language element to be studied. The examples are embedded in whole text and then extracted for closely guided scrutiny. As students scrutinize the parts of language being studied, they are encouraged to form generalizations, find other examples, and discuss any "rules" that they can derive. This part of the lesson makes use of many traditional methods of teaching skills. Finally, students are asked to apply what they know using meaningful, whole texts. This may involve rereading familiar texts or creating new ones.

Instructional Materials

Today's early literacy instruction involves a wide variety of materials and resources for teachers and children. The materials take many forms: traditional print books and magazines, charts and posters, enlarged texts or big books for reading aloud to groups of children with smaller versions that may be used with CD players and headsets by individuals, computer-based technologies. Planning the integrated use of these materials is both exciting and challenging for teachers as they seek to help children acquire and refine their use of phonics and other word study strategies.

Figure 11. Blending Skills With Meaning: A Whole-to-Part-to-Whole Conceptual Framework

---

WHOLE —————to————— PART —————to————— WHOLE

| Learning *with*, *through*, and *about* whole written texts.* | Learning *about* the parts of written language texts. | Applying what was learned *with*, *through*, and *about* whole written language texts. |

Examples of activities

whole	*part*	*whole*
Reading/writing aloud	*Direct instruction*	*Rereading*
Teacher models; students observe and respond.	focuses on selected elements from whole text	Familiar texts

Includes

Shared reading/writing	Phonemic Awareness	*Writing*
Teacher leads; students participate to the extent they can.	Sound/letter patterns for onsets and rimes	Creating alternative texts
	Phonics	Response to reading
	Structural Analysis	
	and	
Guided reading/writing	Other Word Recognition	*Reading*
Teacher engages students in systematic manner with closely guided support.	Strategies (Focus on patterns in sentences, words, word parts, letters, and sounds.)	Applies to new/similar texts (Help is given as needed. Application is monitored.)

---

*Whole texts include predictable stories, dictated stories, content area materials, letters, charts of songs, rhymes, messages, lists, and so on.

Adapted from Strickland, D.S. (1989). *Teaching skills in a literature-based classroom.* Workshop handout distributed at the 34th Annual Convention of the International Reading Association, New Orleans, LA.

Greater Use of a Variety of Materials, Including Trade Books and Library Books

Concern over the use of bland, unmotivating texts for reading instruction, coupled with the availability of more high-quality children's books, led to the introduction of trade books in beginning reading instruction. Although the use of such materials does not preclude a strong phonics emphasis, teachers using trade books as core materials are more likely to capitalize on the opportunities for phonics instruction presented in the literature rather than rely on a rigidly applied hierarchy of skills. Many teachers attempt to blend both approaches by selecting literature that contains the elements they want to teach and then teach them in a *planful* manner. In either case, emphasis is placed on learning phonics in combination with other word identification skills in a context that stimulates children's desire to read. In order to understand the changes that have occurred in the kinds of materials used to teach phonics, it is helpful to have some further background on phonics and instructional materials.

Phonics and Core Reading Programs

Basal or core reading programs produced during the latter part of the 20th century include organized phonics programs. However, because many of these programs made use of a small foundational vocabulary taught as sight words, their approach is termed by some as the *sight-word* or *whole-word* method. According to Heilman (1989), these terms are misnomers, because no current method or philosophy of reading instruction advocates a total sight- or whole-word approach. Although traditional basal readers included phonics instruction, they differed as to the point at which phonics was first introduced, the degree of emphasis on phonics, and the type of phonics used. Differences of this type remain true of today's literature-based, core reading, and language arts programs as well.

Although there are many ways to approach phonics, two different approaches tended to dominate materials and practice in the past. *Synthetic phonics* refers to an approach in which the sounds identified with letters are learned in isolation and blended together. Children are taught to segment a single syllable word such as *cat* into three parts /c/a/t/ and to blend the parts together to form a word. A multisyllable word such as *alphabet* might be segmented as follows: al/pha/bet. *Analytic phonics* refers to an approach in which the sounds associated with letters are not pronounced in isolation. Children identify the phonic element from a set of words in which each word contains the particular element under study. For example, teacher and students discuss how the following words are alike: *pat*, *park*, *push*, and *pen*. Analytic phonics is used in the example given earlier in which a typical basal phonics lesson is described.

Much of the controversy surrounding traditional basal reading programs and phonics centers on disagreements about which of the two approaches, synthetic or analytic, is better. Those who favor instruction with a heavy emphasis on phonics lean toward an explicit or synthetic approach. Many school districts select core reading and language arts programs based on the amount and type of phonics instruction included. The controversy has expanded beyond the type of phonics taught to include issues related to the intensity of instructional delivery and sequence of instruction.

Many teachers purchase supplementary phonics programs to accompany their core literacy programs. Ironically, some teachers may unwittingly contribute to the word recognition problems of marginal students by, for example, pairing a core program using analytic phonics with a supplementary program that uses synthetic phonics. Teachers also may pair a program in which letter names are taught and linked to the sounds they represent with one in which the letters actually are identified by the sounds they represent. For example, teaching that the letter b represents the sound buh is quite different from actually calling that letter buh rather than its letter name. Thus, an instructional mismatch is created that may confuse the children for whom the heavy emphasis on phonics was intended to help.

Beyond the initial levels of reading, traditional basal programs introduced books in the elementary grades that contained stories in which the vocabulary was highly controlled and through which specific language elements were taught in a highly sequenced manner. Teachers often organized primary-grade reading instruction around three ability groups, which allowed students to proceed through the material at varying rates. Assessment consisted primarily of multiple-choice tests given at the completion of each book. Skills such as phonics generally were monitored through worksheet activities.

Following are descriptions that contrast the teaching of phonics as an isolated skill unlinked to meaningful text with the teaching of phonics as a tool grounded in familiar and meaningful text and as part of the entire reading process.

Reexamining the Use of Tightly Controlled, Highly Contrived Texts to Teach Reading

Many adults in the United States learned to read from text such as that shown in Figure 12. Traditional basal readers contained highly controlled

> **Figure 12. Text From a Traditional First-Grade Basal Reader**
>
> See Jack go.
> Go, go Jack.
> Jack can go fast.

vocabulary in stories written for a particular reading series. Books at the beginning levels, preprimers and primers, were designed to introduce children to a limited number of words, which were repeated in several stories. Although the early basals of the 1940s and 1950s included little or no phonics, basals since that time have made use of *sight words* (i.e., words taught as wholes for instant recognition) as the basis for the introduction of phonics. After children had mastered a limited sight vocabulary, sight words and phonics continued to be taught side-by-side.

Most basal phonics programs began by teaching a few consonants in the initial position. Because consonants are much more consistent in their relations to sounds than are vowels, those that represent only one sound (e.g., *m, n, p, b, h, w*) usually were taught early in a sequence of instruction. Having introduced a few such consonants, instruction also would include final consonants, vowels, and structural elements. Although there was a conscious effort to link the phonics lessons to the reading material, these lessons often were taught in a manner that was isolated from real reading. Following are some key elements of a typical phonics lesson that might have occurred within the more eclectic basal readers of the 1970s, 1980s, or 1990s, or in a program used in conjunction with such readers.

Visual Discrimination and Letter Recognition. The teacher displays the uppercase and lowercase forms of the letter under consideration. For example, a key letter card with the letters *Ww* is displayed. Children are told that this is the letter *w*, and they are asked to repeat the name of the letter. In some cases, they also may be asked to use paper and pencil to form or trace the letter.

Auditory Discrimination/Phonemic Awareness. The children are shown a key picture card with the picture of something that begins with the /w/ sound. For example, a picture of a wagon might be used. With heavy stress on the initial sound /w/ in *wagon*, the children are told that the word *wagon* begins with the letter *w*. They are asked to repeat the word in unison and to notice how their lips form at the beginning of the word. Words from their basal vocabulary list such as *we* and *was* also are recalled and compared. A variety of auditory discrimination games might follow.

For example, the teacher might say a list of words and ask whether they begin like *wagon*, *was*, and *we*. In most cases, the teacher would not attempt to isolate the sound of the letter *w*, because it cannot be isolated without distortion. The teacher places emphasis on helping children hear and see the similarity in a given set of words or pictures that stand for words. The goal is for students to become familiar with a specific sound–letter relationship and generalize this knowledge for new situations.

Application. A worksheet with pictures of various objects is distributed to the children. Students are asked to mark all the items that begin with the same sound as the word *wagon*.

Extension. Additional activities might include cutting and pasting pictures of items that begin with the /w/ sound–letter relationship. In addition, a review of all the phonics elements taught would take place over time, both through oral activities and through an abundance of paper and pencil practice tasks.

Assessment. Paper-and-pencil tasks of the type described earlier are used for both instruction and ongoing assessment.

Using Patterned Texts Containing Humor and Lively Illustrations

A good example of a book for use with beginning readers is *I Went Walking* by Sue Williams, a picture book containing repetitive vocabulary and language patterns (see Figure 13). It is beautifully illustrated, simple, and humorous. Following are key points in a series of lessons that might be used with materials of this type.

Modeling. Through numerous shared readings of the book, children are invited to participate as the teacher reads aloud to them. They join in on repeated words and sentences. Children notice how the teacher turns the

> **Figure 13. Text That Can Be Used With Beginning Readers**
>
> I went walking.
> What did you see?
> I saw a black cat looking at me.
>
> I went walking.
> What did you see?
> I saw a brown horse looking at me.
>
> Excerpt from *I Went Walking*, copyright © 1989 by Sue Williams, reproduced by permission of Houghton Mifflin Harcourt Publishing Company.

pages and how his or her hand occasionally sweeps from left to right or top to bottom, indicating where the written message is located and the direction in which his or her eyes are moving.

Repeated Readings and Response. Children respond to repeated readings of the text in a variety of ways, such as discussion, drama, and drawing and writing.

Identifying Textual Features. After several readings, children are guided to look more closely at the textual features. They may match sentences in the book with sentences the teacher has written on a strip of oak tag. They may reconstruct sentences that have been cut into individual words.

Phonics. As children become more familiar with the text, they are guided to notice the words beginning with the letter *w* that are repeated throughout the book in the sentences *I went walking. What did you see?* They match the words visually, read them in unison, and discuss the sound–letter relationship.

Using the Language of Literacy. Throughout these activities, both teacher and children use the language of literacy. Vocabulary such as *letter, word, sentence, period, author,* and *illustrator* are used in context so that students attain the vocabulary needed to learn and talk about what they read and write.

Application. Whole-group activities using the Big Book version of texts such as *I Went Walking* are accompanied by opportunities for independent reading of the smaller version of the Big Book at school and at home.

Children also are engaged in many traditional phonics activities with the letter *w*, such as creating a chart of pictures of things that begin with the letter *w*. Through daily independent writing opportunities, such as journal writing or written responses to literature, children are encouraged to apply all the sound–letter relationships that have been taught.

Assessment. Assessment is highly integrated with instruction. Ongoing informal classroom assessment of children's participation in whole-group activities and their independent reading and writing helps determine the children who need additional help. Children are held accountable for skills and strategies that have been addressed through direct and indirect instruction. Teachers also look for evidence of students' risk taking as they attempt to apply what they have learned to sound–letter relationships that have not been addressed specifically. Teachers are less concerned with teaching each specific letter in a particular sequence than in helping children develop an awareness of the alphabetic principle and an understanding of how this knowledge can help them read and write. Emphasis is placed on guiding children to make their own personal discoveries of how their language system works so that they can use this knowledge to generalize to new situations. That is, the ultimate goal is to teach so that students can use what they have learned in similar but new contexts.

This lesson grounds instruction in authentic literature and requires students to use the phonics element being studied in a meaningful and strategic manner. This lesson also could be described as a blend of implicit (or embedded) instruction with explicit instruction. Making use of a whole-to-part-to-whole framework, described in Figure 11, the teacher begins by immersing children in examples of the pattern underlying the skill or strategy they are studying (the letter *w* sound–symbol relationship) in the hope that they will begin to discover it on their own.

However, whether they discover the pattern themselves, students are guided to look closely at how it exists in whole text. Once the pattern is discussed, it is removed from the context and is given more intense and explicit scrutiny. Finally, students are given opportunities to use what they know about the pattern in their reading and spelling, and they are held accountable for it. The teacher is given an opportunity to discover whether children have truly learned what has been taught and to tailor future lessons accordingly.

Making Use of Multimedia Technologies

In recent years, teachers have increased their use of a variety of technologies in support of literacy learning. The use of software programs in classroom computer centers is common. Researchers have turned their attention to the values and cautions regarding the use of these materials. For example, research indicates that listening to electronic stories, while watching animations and text unfold on the computer screen, helps young children acquire various aspects of literacy, including knowledge of sight words and concepts about print (Labbo & Kuhn, 2000). Nevertheless, researchers warn that many Internet sites that supposedly provide young learners with suitable literacy activities are not developmentally appropriate. It is important for educators to seek current, reliable, and objective information regarding the use of technology in the classroom. Recommended Internet sites and materials can be obtained by consulting journal articles and other resources such as Labbo (2006) and Wasburn-Moses (2006).

Many teachers now are constructing their own program of strategies for phonics instruction or augmenting the core program selected by the school or district. They select the literature themselves and offer phonics

A young student engages in a computer-based reading activity.

instruction much like the series of lessons described in this chapter. This trend also is reflected in some commercially prepared materials for beginning reading. However, in an attempt to please a wide variety of consumers, publishers of literature-based programs are likely to include options that reflect more than one approach to teaching phonics. They may differ, however, in the amount of phonics offered prior to actual book-reading experiences.

Programs that espouse a phonics-first approach will expose children to heavy doses of intensive phonics before much instruction is offered with books and stories. This is in contrast to programs in which phonics is more closely linked to the literature selections that children read from the beginning. For the most part, however, commercially prepared materials are less likely to reflect one strong philosophical base, because their goal is to provide something for everyone. Whether teacher prepared or commercially published, there is one thing of which you can be assured: Today's reading programs will include phonics.

Greater Reliance on Informal Classroom Assessment

Although many still consider standardized tests the chief indicator of student achievement, classroom teachers are beginning to make greater use of informal assessment procedures to inform them about student progress. Teachers have come to realize that standardized tests tell them very little about a specific child's strengths and weaknesses. These tests usually are given at the end of the year, rendering the results useless for instructional purposes. Some teachers complain that standardized tests do not accurately reflect what they have emphasized instructionally. Still others observe that young children sometimes are overwhelmed by the format of these tests, which often is very different from the kinds of literacy materials they use on a daily basis. Teachers have gathered evidence from workbooks and worksheets, but this, too, is not always satisfactory, because some children can function well on these materials and still have difficulty applying skills.

Today's teachers seek to obtain information about how students use word identification tools, such as phonics, when they are involved in reading and writing for their own purposes. They are aware that the best test of knowledge is its application during use. Observing children's application of phonics is the best indicator of how well they have learned it and the best basis for differentiating instruction according to students' needs. The examples of record keeping in Chapter 2, Figure 6, show how effective teachers gather and examine children's work samples in order to make thoughtful instructional decisions.

Balancing Teacher–Based Classroom Assessment With Commercially Prepared Assessment Tools

Formal, standardized testing of young learners' foundational reading skills is relatively recent. For many years, the primary way to evaluate how well students had learned phonics was through a demonstration of knowledge about sound–letter relationships. Most often this was done by observing performance during instructional activities and on worksheets like the one shown in Figure 14. To be sure, when a child circles the letter *d* under a picture of a dog to indicate the sound it represents at the beginning, we know that this child is making some very valuable connections. It tells us little, however, about the child's ability to use this information in the act of reading and writing. Teachers have observed that children's requirements on skills sheets can pose a very different challenge from the strategic use of phonics required when they actually read and write.

Increasingly common in today's schools is the administration of standardized tests, such as the Dynamic Indicators of Basic Early Literacy Skills (see Hintze, Ryan, & Stone, 2003). The increased use of such tests is a reflection of national and state policies designed to encourage systematic progress monitoring. Unfortunately, while such tests are useful as screening or diagnostic instruments, their impact on expectations for comprehension growth is probably limited. Moreover, their limited emphasis on comprehension is likely to influence the day-to-day parsing of reading instruction and the interim expectations for students' achievement—something that is discongruent with third-grade expectations for reading achievement (Salinger, 2006). Focusing on enabling skills "can shape expectations for students' learning, obscuring the fact that what will ultimately be measured is application of a unified body of strategies and skills orchestrated to make sense out of continuous text" (p. 435). Policies that encourage a mixed and more informed use of standardized and classroom assessments that inform daily practice are needed.

Figure 14. Sample Phonics Worksheet

Write Dd next to all of the things that begin with the same sound as dog.

Using Teacher–Prepared, Ongoing Assessment Strategies for Instructional Decision–Making

Many school districts have reduced the number of norm-referenced tests given before third grade. These have been replaced with a variety of performance-based assessment procedures that are linked closely to the curriculum. For example, teachers may use some form of running record of the types of errors children make during oral reading (see Clay, 1989;

Leslie & Caldwell, 1995). This type of assessment helps the teacher go beyond merely recording the number of errors made to noting the *type* of errors made.

For example, when a child makes a reading error, it may be due to a lack of attention to one of several cues to word recognition. In Figure 15, the reader says *call* for *calm*, indicating a lack of attention to what makes sense in this context. Use of the word *came* also should signal a sense of discomfort in the reader; it neither makes sense nor is its use "the way we say it" (English sentence structure) in our language. *Clean* for *calm* indicates use of the visual elements in *calm* in an attempt to apply phonics. But the learner must go beyond the visual and think in terms of what makes sense and what sounds correct in our language. The type of errors readers make will suggest the type of prompts that should be offered and will determine the kind of follow-up instruction required.

Observing and monitoring children's attempts at spelling during writing is another invaluable window into their ability to use phonics. The analysis in Figure 9 is an example of how a teacher might assess phonics within the instructional context. Teachers look for the application of skills already taught as well as attempts that go beyond the instruction already received. This helps to indicate what a child is ready for next. Work samples of this type also provide specific, concrete evidence for use during parent conferences. Today's teachers find it much more helpful to spend time with parents reviewing their child's work samples and records gleaned from checklists and observational notes than merely discussing standardized test

Figure 15. All Reading Errors Are Not Equal

Example:
A picture of a mother bathing a child is accompanied by the following sentence:
Mother tried to calm *the crying baby.*

Error	Possible prompt	Type of error
call for *calm*	semantic (meaning)	Does that make sense?
came for *calm*	syntax (sentence structure)	Does that sound right?
clean for *calm*	graphophonic (sound–letter)	It could be, but look again.

results. Products and observations from instructional activities provide a vivid and accurate description of an individual's personal progress.

New insights into young children's literacy development have led to changes in beginning reading instruction. The insights not only stem from recent research, but they also are grounded in research of the past that is now better understood and put to better use. For example, knowledge about the writing process and its relation to reading has led to new understandings about how young children's early writing can promote the development of phonics. It also reveals how children's attempts to spell can be used to monitor what they know about phonics as well as how they put this knowledge to use. Perhaps more than ever before, today's teachers are apt to blend phonics into an instructional framework that emphasizes the reader's construction of meaning with texts. In this way, students are encouraged to use phonics as a tool toward making sense of what they read rather than as an end in itself.

IDEA TO THINK AND TALK ABOUT

1. Discuss the trends outlined in this chapter. Compare them with an early literacy program with which you are familiar. What are the similarities and differences? What things concern you the most?

CHAPTER 4

Finding the Balance: Systematic, Intensive, Code-Driven Phonics Versus Holistic, Embedded, Meaning-Driven Approaches

The discussion of the controversies surrounding phonics is not complete without addressing the issues as they are likely to appear in their most extreme form—the debate surrounding systematic, intensive phonics versus holistically oriented approaches. This is the form in which the controversy most likely is to be cast to the general public. The distinction between these two approaches is most significant at the very earliest point of formal instruction in reading. This chapter provides the background required to make thoughtful and informed curriculum choices.

Stated briefly, educators who promote systematic, intensive phonics advocate an emphasis on phonics that is highly sequenced, skills- or code-driven, and initiated early in the child's schooling. Children begin by learning about the parts of words and build toward whole words. Correct identification and automaticity of response is stressed. Much of the research cited to support this view is grounded in experimental studies in which children's demonstration of performance is based on the results of standardized tests (Adams, 1990; Chall, 1983).

Holistically oriented approaches include philosophies and practices frequently associated with terms such as *whole language*, *integrated language arts*, and *literature-based curricula*. In practice, these terms share certain characteristics; however, they are not synonymous. For example, the trends in literacy education outlined in Chapter 3 (i.e., greater emphasis on writing and its relation to reading; increased attention to the integration of all the language arts; greater use of a variety of materials, including trade books and library books; and greater reliance on informal classroom assessment) are visible in virtually all classrooms where a holistic orientation

A teacher observes and listens as a student reads independently.

is espoused. However, implementation and adherence to various philosophies varies widely from teacher to teacher. To make matters more confusing, teachers who support intensive, systematic phonics often include some of the instructional elements considered to be holistic in nature.

In a discussion of phonics, the distinction between an explicit code or skills emphasis (i.e., systematic, intensive phonics) and an embedded code or meaning emphasis (i.e., reading- and writing-based phonics) rests in how reading is taught from the very beginning. Advocates of reading- and writing-based phonics focus on instruction that is embedded within the processes of learning to read and write and emphasize the child's ability to make meaning with text. Children begin with the use of whole texts involving shared literacy activities with an adult and move to the identification of phrases and words and the examination of word parts. Emphasis on meaning is maintained even as children examine word parts, because the purpose is to help them see the patterns in the language so they can apply the knowledge to new situations. Those who endorse a meaning emphasis are likely to cite basic research on how children learn to read and write as well as classroom-based studies on long-term effects of reading- and writing-based phonics (Krashen, 1993; Weaver, 1994).

Recognizing that in most controversies there is something to be learned from both sides, I have attempted in this book to avoid extremes on the phonics debate. For example, educators on both sides of the debate agree that, ultimately, reading and writing for meaning is paramount. Both sides are keenly aware of the importance of good literature in the lives of children and the need for responsive adults who support children's natural inclinations toward making sense of print.

Both sides of the phonics debate could learn from educators in Finland. Because the Finnish language is said to be the most regular alphabetic writing system in use today (Venezky, 1973), it is not surprising that educators there turned to synthetic phonics as the major instructional approach to beginning reading. It also is not surprising that Finnish researchers report that phonics instruction decreased poor readers' decoding problems in the first grade. "Even the students with low IQs can learn fluent mechanical reading skills" (Korkeamaki & Dreher, 1993, p. 478). However, the jump start in phonics given to Finnish children has not created a country free of reading problems. Studies suggest that a large proportion of Finnish children have serious problems with reading comprehension: 20% in Grade 3 (Vähäpassi, 1977a), 50% in Grade 6 (Vähäpassi, 1977b), and 30% in Grade 9 (Vähäpassi, 1987).

These findings parallel Venezky's (1973) finding that although Finnish students achieve a surprisingly high level of sound–letter mastery by the end of first grade, only 25% of the variation in the students' reading ability in the second and third grades could be attributed to the mastery of sound–letter correspondence. It could be that for many learners, an instructional program (in any discipline) that is devoid of meaning and purpose produces mindless, quick results at the expense of long-term strategies for independence and self-improvement. This should not be viewed as an indictment of phonics; rather, it is an indictment of how phonics was taught in this situation. The questions educators and parents face regarding phonics never has been about whether to teach it, but about how much phonics to teach, to whom, and at what time.

Educators who seek to provide a comprehensive and balanced instructional program would do well to consider the following:

- Instruction is systematic when it is planned, deliberate in application, and proceeds in an orderly manner. This does not mean a rigid progression of "one-size-fits-all" instruction. Rather, it means a thoughtfully planned program that takes into account learner variability.

- The intensity of instruction on any particular skill or strategy should be based on need. Thus, intensity will vary both with individuals and groups. There is no substitute for ongoing documentation and monitoring of learning in order to determine the level of intensity needed to help a child or group of children succeed in a particular area.

- The use of techniques to track specific goals and objectives within an integrated language arts framework is essential. Alignment of curricular goals with instructional planning and assessment helps provide everyone involved with a clear sense of direction. Instruction should be engaging and rich with meaning, yet grounded in curricular expectations that are visible to teachers, parents, students, and concerned others.

- Instructional techniques that help children understand and make use of the alphabetic code should be applied with those that guide students in reading comprehension, thoughtful response to literature, and the effective use of the writing process.

Avoiding instructional extremes is at the heart of providing a balanced program of reading instruction. However, finding the balance should not imply that there is a specific balanced approach. Nor should it suggest a sampling method in which "a little of this and a little of that" are mixed together to form a disparate grouping of approaches euphemistically termed "eclectic." Ultimately, instruction must be informed by how children learn and how they can best be taught. Achieving informed balance is an ongoing endeavor that requires knowledge, time, and thoughtfulness (Strickland, 2004).

IDEA TO THINK AND TALK ABOUT

1. Most educators advocate for *balance* in the literacy curriculum. What does the term *balance* mean to you? Share some ideas about how it might be achieved in the areas of curriculum, instruction, and assessment.

CHAPTER 5

Strategies for Beginning Readers and Writers and Those Needing Additional Support and Intervention

Learning phonics is not something children do in a vacuum. It occurs within the context of family and school environments that influence whether children are successful. Virtually all children come to school having had some exposure to print during their daily lives; however, the nature and extent of this exposure varies widely. It is no surprise that children's ability to learn phonics is related to the frequency and quality of their informal experiences with written and oral language.

The concepts presented in this chapter provide a foundation for phonics and continue to develop along with phonics. Children begin to develop these concepts at home and in school settings with early childhood caregivers and teachers. They learn best when the adults who care for them *plan* for the activities and experiences to happen in relatively informal and meaningful ways rather than rely on a set of rigidly prescribed and sometimes mindless formal lessons.

This chapter begins by placing phonics and word study instruction within the broader frame of literacy learning and teaching. Understanding the variability among learners is acknowledged as a key part of ensuring their success. Without differentiated instruction many learners will not benefit from initial instruction. Others will need remediation and intervention long after the beginning stages. Specific strategies are provided for various aspects of word study instruction in the early grades and for intervention with learners who need additional support well beyond the early grade levels. The strategies may be adapted to suit learners at any point of need.

Strategies for Developing the Foundations of Reading and Writing

Print awareness involves an understanding that reading and writing represent ideas, knowledge, and thoughts. Attention to print is an important first step toward developing an understanding of what it means to be a reader and writer, even though it may or may not predict an ease of understanding the relations between the sounds and symbols of written language. Adults promote children's print awareness by providing print-rich environments and by being responsive to young children's questions and comments about print.

Print concepts are the arbitrary conventions that govern written language, such as spaces between words, directionality, and punctuation. Developing an understanding of how print works is essential to make sense of written language. Adults promote an understanding of print concepts when they move their hand from left to right while reading a familiar phrase or sentence, point to individual words to help children associate the spoken and written forms, call attention to the need to put spaces between words while writing a note or list dictated by a child, and respond to children's questions about periods or question marks they have noticed during reading or writing.

Functions of print involves knowledge of how print is used for everyday purposes, such as writing notes and letters, reading newspapers and magazines, making and using lists, and using a television guide. Children who realize the functional relevance of written language are more likely to be motivated to explore its use for their own purposes. Adults include children in functional activities involving print, such as clipping coupons from a supermarket circular, writing a note to a friend, writing a list of things to do, and reading a menu at a restaurant.

Knowledge of narrative structure involves understanding the nature of stories and how they are constructed. Knowledge of the structure of stories is important, because most of the material used to teach reading to young children is written in narrative form. Children are likely to understand material presented in a form with which they are familiar. Reading and rereading storybooks aloud to children is one of the best ways to build a sense of stories. Storytelling by adults and children is entertaining and is a natural way to reinforce and extend children's conceptions of how

A teacher guides students as they analyze and discuss a new word.

characters, plot, setting, and other story elements work together to form narratives.

Literacy as a source of enjoyment refers to the development of a positive attitude toward reading and other literacy experiences. Children who have positive attitudes and expectations about reading are more likely to be motivated to learn to read. Adults can share books of all types: stories, informational books, and poetry. This is one of the best ways to promote a sense that reading is fun. Books that contain humor and language play provide enjoyment while fostering a sensitivity to language. Anyone who reads the title is not surprised that Joseph Slate's rhyming animal alphabet story, *Miss Bindergarten Gets Ready for Kindergarten* is a big hit with young children. Having paper, writing instruments, and books available for children's pretend play and independent exploration allows them to explore these materials on their own terms. Drawing and writing often become an integral part of pretending as children explore their use for self-expression.

Extending vocabulary and language patterns involves the development of vocabulary and linguistic patterns children need to make good predictions about print. This book emphasizes the idea that making sense of print requires the use of a combination of semantic, syntactic, and graphophonic cues along with background knowledge. Children who have an abundance of opportunities to expand their language and linguistic repertoires are more apt to recognize words unknown to them as readers and to make sense of what they read. Participation in read-aloud activities in family and school situations and in interesting talk at school and at the family dinner table appear to have a major influence on children's language abilities and their background knowledge.

Strategies That Support Learning the Alphabet

Although children's ability to recognize the letters of the alphabet is an excellent predictor of first- and second-grade reading achievement, this knowledge probably reflects more about a child's general knowledge about books and print than the fact that he or she can name letters. In fact, children do not need to know all of the letters of the alphabet or know them in any particular order before they begin learning to read and write. The best practice is to help children identify letters and numbers in an enjoyable way as they acquire the broader concepts about print and books they will need as a foundation for literacy. The following are some tips:

- Focus on letters that have special meaning for children, such as the letters in their own names. This is more effective than simply teaching one arbitrary letter per week.
- Teach the alphabet song. This is fun for children, and it gives them something to rely on when they attempt to use simple dictionaries or try to locate particular letters on alphabet charts.
- Post children's names in places that will help them identify them. Point occasionally to the letters, spelling children's names for them.
- Print each letter of a child's name on separate cards or pieces of paper. Scramble them and let the child reconstruct his or her name as he or she matches the cut-up version to a complete one.
- Read alphabet books on a regular basis and make them available for children to browse through on their own. Encourage children to work with a buddy and read together.

- Encourage children to experiment with letter forms. Use clay, finger paint, chalk and chalkboard, felt and sandpaper letters, alphabet puzzles, and wood and magnetic letters.

- Keep alphabet charts at children's eye level so that they can be referred to easily.

- Place children's names on index cards or place them in a pocket chart so that they can be removed and read closely. Use only a few names at a time. Ask children to locate their own names, find the names that start with the same letter or end with the same letter, and identify a particular letter that you display.

- Make simple picture dictionaries available.

- Help children make a class alphabet book or an individual alphabet book.

Strategies That Support Phonemic Awareness

Activities promoting phonemic awareness help children perceive their language as a series of sounds that they can pay attention to, segment, and categorize. Activities should be playful and game-like, much like the way children manipulate the language of songs, chants, and rhymes on their own. Keep the atmosphere informal and avoid putting children under any stress, which might make them retreat from participating and thus do more harm than good. Here are some ideas:

- Include nursery rhymes, poems, and storybooks with patterned rhymes in your daily read-aloud repertoire.

- Read poetry and stories that contain alliteration and word play, including alphabet books.

- Pause before a rhyming word and let children fill in the rhyme when reading or chanting a familiar poem or rhyme.

- Create your own simple rhymes and invite children to try some as well.

- Encourage and praise children's self-initiated attempts to memorize very simple rhymes and songs.

- Make or purchase games that feature rhyming words when children are familiar with the concept of rhyme. Children may match pictures that rhyme or they may use a bingo-type game board to cover pictures that rhyme with one drawn from the box.

- Invite children to clap the number of syllables they hear in someone's name. First say the name, then repeat it with the children as they clap with you; John gets one clap, Mary gets two, Jonathan gets three, and so on.

- Help children to identify similarities in sounds. Model the following in a sing-song manner:

  > *Ball* is a word that starts like *boy.*
  > Boy/ball, boy/ball.
  >
  > Can you think of a word that starts like *boy?*

  When a child responds correctly (for example, *Bill*) repeat the following:

  > *Bill* is a word that starts like *boy.*
  > Boy/Bill, boy/Bill.
  >
  > Can you think of a word that starts like *boy?*

  Encourage children to join subsequent rounds. After they grasp the idea, consider moving on to medial and final sounds. Keep the words simple and stress the sound clearly as well as its placement in the word (i.e., beginning, medial, end).

- Determine when children have a sense of what it means to attend to component sounds in words. Then, invite them to try the following: Slowly stretch the sounds of short words with two or three sounds, such as *see* (two sounds), *cat* (three sounds), or *dish* (three sounds). As you say each word, push a penny, small tile, or blank card forward for each sound heard: /c/ is one sound; /a/ is two; /t/ is three. Model this several times before you ask children to try it. Encourage children to use this stretching technique when they are attempting to spell words on their own.

Strategies That Support Phonics

The instructional activities recommended in support of phonemic awareness also relate directly to phonics. Additional strategies follow:

- Take advantage of opportunities to discuss interesting sound–letter patterns in literature that you are reading aloud. Keep in mind that during the first or second reading of a book or story, it is best to respond to the content. That is, discuss the plot, characters, and ideas for information and enjoyment. After that, you may want to ask children if they have noticed anything special about certain words. Help them to establish the relations among words or parts of words that look and sound alike. Encourage this kind of observation of written language in reading and writing activities throughout the day.

- Invite children to watch as you write messages and lists. Think aloud as you model the use of phonics to help with spelling. For example, say, "We need to make a list of the things we need to plant our seeds." Emphasizing the /d/, say, "*Dirt* starts just like *dog*. I need to start with a *d*." You will not do this with *every* word or letter, but do enough so that children get the idea of how writers think when they spell. As children become knowledgeable about phonics, call on them to help when you think aloud. Let them tell the part they know as you fill in the rest.

- Use children's names to point out similarities and differences in the way they look and sound. Choose pairs such as *Jamal* and *Jennifer*. Have children notice how they look and sound alike at the beginning, middle, and end.

- Encourage children's attempts to write. Most often, the writing gradually moves from scribbling and forming strings of letters to an attempt to represent sounds with letters. When this occurs, encourage children to stretch the word, thinking about the way it sounds and the letter(s) that come to mind. Some children aim for correctness from the beginning. Give help, but let them know how much you value their own attempts. Encourage children to write the part they do know and leave the rest for your help later. Writing the sounds they hear helps children internalize phonics. Make special attempts to acknowledge a child's thoughtful reasoning when his or her attempts appear logical to the child but produce unconventional spellings. For example, it would seem logical to begin the word *city* with an *s* or *truck* with *chr* at the beginning—most young children pronounce it this way. As young children sort through these things, they need to know that their attempts are valued and show their ability as thinkers.

- Use the opportunity of a child's query about a word to point out sound–letter relationships: "This one begins with *s*. It says *salt*. This one begins with *p* and says *pepper*."

- Avoid immediately telling children the words they do not know or read incorrectly as you listen to them read. You might ask them to think about what makes sense and then look at the word together to sound it out. Help children divide words into manageable chunks rather than sounding out words letter by letter.

- Involve children in word making activities (Cunningham & Cunningham, 1992) in which children are guided in creating words from letters they are given. During this 15-minute activity, children make 12 to 15 words, beginning with two-letter words and continuing with three-, four-, five-letter, and longer words until the final word is made. The final word (a six-, seven-, or eight-letter word) always contains all the letters they have that day. For example, from the word *spider*, children are guided in making the words *Ed, red, rid, sip, pie, pies, dies, side, ride, ripe, rise, pride*, and *drips*. Start by allowing children to work in small groups or pairs. Give constant feedback.

- Involve children in various sorting activities. Play games that require them to sort pictures into categories according to their beginning, medial, or ending sounds. Word sorting involves categorizing words with the same rhyming families, vowel generalizations, or other language pattern under study. Children enjoy manipulating picture cards and word cards. In contrast to worksheets, sorting involves children with a large number of examples and requires them to think analytically and critically. Simply adjust the level of the activity to the children's level of development (Bear, Invernizzi, Templeton, & Johnston, 1996; Ganske, 2000).

- Develop a strategy of predicting, using multiple cueing systems. Using a familiar selection, choose a word and cover it with your finger or a piece of paper. Or simply write a sentence, covering one word. Ask children to predict what words might fit in the empty slot. Write down each word as it is given. If a child offers a word that does not make sense, discuss it. At this point, they are using semantic and syntactic cues. Uncover the first letter of the word. With the children's help, go through the list, eliminating each word that will not fit now that they have more information. Now they have added phonics to the decoding cues they are using. Finally, uncover the whole word and examine it with the children to confirm or correct their predictions. The following is an example of this process:

> The sentence is, "*Bill likes to eat ___ (pizza).*"
> The children offer *hot dogs*, *ice cream*, *hamburgers*, *steak*. The teacher lists the words given.
> The first letter is uncovered, and it is the letter *p*.
> The children go through the list, only to discover that none of the words fit.
> The children list new words. Now they should only give words beginning with the letter *p*.
> The word is uncovered so that they can confirm or correct their predictions.
>
> (Note: If the word begins with a consonant blend, uncover the blend rather than just the first consonant.)

Strategies That Support Onset–Rime Analogies

Keep in mind that the analogy strategy is limited by the knowledge of onsets and rimes learners have stored in their memory. For example, a learner who does not have the word *can* stored in his or her memory will be unable to use the analogy strategy to identify the word *pan*. Obviously, the greater the number of words with varied rimes learners have in their reading vocabularies, the more useful the analogy strategy. Wylie and Durrell (1970) identify 37 phonograms that could be found in almost 500 primary-grade words. These high-utility phonograms are *ack, ail, ain, ake, ale, ame, an, ank, ap, ash, at, ate, aw, ay, eat, ell, est, ice, ick, ide, ight, ill, in, ine, ing, ink, ip, it, ock, oke, op, ore, ot, uck, ug, ump,* and *unk*. This is a useful list for generating activities. Suggested activities follow:

- Play simple consonant-substitution games: Start with a known word such as *cat*. Using the chalkboard, demonstrate what happens when the *c* in *cat* is substituted for other consonants. You might find it helpful to chant the following in a sing-song manner:

You take the *c* away from *cat*, put in *p* and you get *pat*.
You take the *p* away from *pat*, put in *f* and you get *fat*.

Continue in this manner, making as many words as you can that children are likely to have in their listening vocabularies. After the children have caught on, pause before saying the new word and see if they can identify it. Continue doing the same with other known words with high-utility phonograms.

- Identify a known word, and have students generate as many words as they can that rhyme with it. Write down each word. Guide children to notice the similarities. For example, say, "Here is the word *ride*. Can you think of words that rhyme with *ride*?" When a rhyming word does not conform to the spelling pattern, simply write it down. Guide children to notice the difference. Then move that word into another column to show that it gets sorted differently.

- Tell students, "I am thinking of a word." Say, "It begins like *ball* and rhymes with *tack*. What could it be?" Have children guess orally first. After they have caught on, have them write the word independently and then share what they have written. Remember to stick to words that are within the children's listening vocabularies. Using nonsense words or words with which they are unfamiliar may confuse children, rather than help them link these activities to real reading.

- Guide children to use onset–rime analogies with other word identification strategies linked to meaning. Write a sentence on the board, such as *Mother put the _____ on the table*. It begins like *dog* and rhymes with *wish*. What could it be?

The following activity is designed for learners who have experienced difficulty in their initial attempt at learning to read. Involve children in word study activities in which they work closely with words, segmenting them, analyzing them, and discussing them. This kind of activity not only makes the patterns in language visible, but it also helps children store the fully analyzed words into their memories for use in forming analogies. Gaskins, Ehri, Cress, O'Hara, and Donnelly (1996) and Ganske (2000) suggest that teachers model and provide guided practice in self-talk strategies similar to the one following, which was designed to help students learn words containing rimes for use with onset–rime analogies:

The teacher begins by giving the word orally. This makes it easier for students to focus on the sounds:

1. The word is _____.
2. Stretch the word. I hear _____ sounds.

Students are shown the word, and it is analyzed in terms of what students already know about language patterns. For example:

3. I see _____ letters because _____.
4. The spelling pattern is _____.
5. This is what I know about the vowel: _____.
6. A word that rhymes with this one is _____.

Or, another word on the word wall* with the same vowel sound is _____.

(*The word wall consists of a list of keywords that are high-frequency words in English and have common spelling patterns. The words are posted for all to view.)

Learning to read is not something that begins in first grade or starts with memorizing the alphabet. From infancy, children are emerging as literate human beings. Virtually everything they learn about language and about their world contributes to their becoming literate. The everyday activities during which children observe adults using print to accomplish tasks and in which children involve literacy in their play are among the most powerful literacy lessons a child can have. Sharing books and engaging in interesting conversations with responsive adults provide the foundation for children's interest in learning to read. These experiences stimulate children's curiosity and inform and motivate their personal explorations with print.

Strategies That Support Conventional Spelling

Encouraging children to develop confidence in expressing their thoughts through writing is a key goal of literacy instruction. They should be encouraged to express their ideas and to take risks in spelling words as best they can. Children also need continuing support in their ability to move toward conventional spelling so that others may read what they are attempting to convey. Creating an atmosphere of interest and discussion about words—both in terms of their meanings and how they are formed— will go a long way toward this end. Following are suggestions for focusing children's attention to how words are formed:

- Select certain words that contain elements of interest after reading and prompt children to share and discuss what they notice.
- Teach children the correct spelling of high-frequency words. This may require small-group, differentiated instruction for those who need it.
- Encourage children to circle words they are unsure of in early drafts of their writing and then seek spelling assistance from others.
- Have children keep personal spelling journals in which words are organized alphabetically. In addition to the regular spelling tests required of all students, selected words from these journals may be used to differentiate and personalize spelling assessments according to need.

During writing, teach children to use the following strategies when attempting to spell a word:

1. Say the word softly to yourself while thinking of the sounds you hear.
2. Attempt to write the word.
3. Take a second look and make any changes you feel are needed.
4. Circle the word if you are still unsure and go on with your writing.
5. Check the correct spelling when you are finished with your writing.
6. Get help from others (if necessary) and correct the spelling on your work, then enter it into your spelling journal.

Strategies That Support ELs

It is important to note that while the specific needs of ELs are beyond the purview of this book, the strategies offered here are relevant to these children. According to Yopp and Stapleton (2008), although much of the research on the relationship between phonemic awareness and reading has been conducted with English monolinguals, a growing body of evidence indicates the relationship holds true for speakers of other languages as well, particularly alphabetic languages.

Shanahan and Beck (2006) examine studies that involved ELs in the five critical components identified in the National Reading Panel report (i.e., phonemic awareness, phonics, vocabulary development, comprehension, fluency). They conclude that instruction in these components generally benefits ELs. However, they also point out that these benefits have been smaller for ELs than for Native Speakers.

The evidence suggests that attention to ELs' phonemic awareness and phonics is worthwhile whether the children are in classrooms where the language of reading instruction is their native language or English. In addition, there is no evidence that phonemic awareness and phonics instruction in English needs to be delayed until a certain threshold of English oral language proficiency is attained (Manyak & Bauer, 2008). Following are suggestions for adaptations and modifications to meet the needs of ELs:

- Learn as much as you can about the common points of difference between English and the other languages used by your students. This will help you understand why children respond as they do and what "rules" they are operating under. It also enables you to respond appropriately. Table 1 will be helpful to teachers who are working with students whose home language is Spanish.

- Make strategic use of children's home language in order to call attention to the similarities and differences between English and Spanish (or other home languages).

- Help children hear English sounds that do not exist or are not salient in their home language.

- Plan and organize the day in order to provide time for extra support and practice.

- Maintain consistent expectations, instruction, and routines.

Strategies That Support Differentiated Instruction

As with all areas of literacy development, students vary in their acquisition of phonics and word study skills. As indicated in Chapter 3, today's teachers designate large blocks of time specifically for English language arts instruction every day. This large block of time is divided between whole-group and small-group instruction, allowing teachers to systematically introduce grade-level skills and strategies to the entire class and also attend to the specific needs of individuals and small groups. Differentiated instruction is essential to the prevention of reading difficulties and provides

Table 1. Some Differences Between the English and Spanish Sound Systems

English Form	Spanish Equivalent	For the Spanish-English Pronunciation of: _____ the Child May Say _____ or to the English Speaker ____ Sounds Like ____	
\i\	\ē\	bit	beet
		pit	peat
\a\	\e\	bat	bet
\a\	\ä\	hat	hot
\ə\	\e\ or \a\	but	bet
\ə\	\ó\	fun	fawn
		shut	shot
\a\	\e\	late	let
		mate	met
\ú\	\ü\	full	fool
\b\	\p\	bar	par
		cab	cap
\b\ (between vowels)	\v\	babies	bavies
\v\	\b\	vote	boat
\sh\	\ch\	shoe	chew
\g\	\k\	goat	coat
		dug	duck
\j\	\ch\ or \y\	jump	chump
			yump
\m\ (final)	\n\	comb	cone
		dime	dine
\th\ (voiceless)	\s\,\t\, or \f\	thank	sank
		path	pass
\th\ (voiced)	\d\	this	dis
		though	dough
\w\	\gw\	way	guay
\z\	\s\	zoo	sue
		buzz	bus
\zh\	\ch\ \sh\	measure	meachure
			meashure

Note. An adaptation by Robert Ruddell in *Reading-Language Instruction: Innovation Practices*, pp. 273–274. © 1974 by Prentice Hall, Inc.

for the intervention needed for those who require extra support (Strickland, Ganske, & Monroe, 2002). Differentiated instruction requires the following:

• Daily planning, involving strategic reading and writing and word study for the whole group followed by teacher-directed, small-group instruction with parallel independent reading and writing activities by students working alone, in pairs, or in small groups. The constituency of the small groups will vary over time.

- Center-based and small-group activities that serve as a follow-up to the suggestions in this chapter. These may include word study games and activities involving letter recognition, word building, and independent reading and writing.

- The regular classroom provides the first level of intervention for students who need extra help. Special intervention by reading specialists and others may sometimes be required, but it should not substitute for daily differentiated and focused intervention within the frame of regular instruction.

Teachers can select from a wide variety of instructional activities to promote students' phonemic awareness, knowledge and use of phonics, the use of onset–rime analogies, and their progress toward conventional spelling. In selecting activities, teachers must be mindful of the age and developmental levels of students, the need to keep instruction engaging for young learners, and the need to create a context that allows children to make connections between the activities in which they are engaged and their use in meaningful literacy acts.

IDEAS TO THINK AND TALK ABOUT

1. Discuss the strategies offered in this chapter. In what ways are they similar to strategies you use or know about? How are they different? Discuss any curriculum changes you might make.

2. Reflect on a typical day in a classroom with which you are familiar. Is there an attempt to meet the varied needs of students? If so, how does differentiation take place?

CHAPTER 6

Shaping Curriculum:
Linking Standards, Instruction,
and Assessment

High standards for student achievement have become the basis for reform at national, state, and local levels. A broadly stated standard such as "Students will read and respond effectively to a variety of types of texts" is intended as a general guideline for educators K–12. However, the statement must be expanded on to provide a framework for instruction at specific grade levels. In the case of word identification, teachers of beginning reading want to know what students should know and be able to do in order to meet the standard.

For example, the *Common Core State Standards for English Language Arts & Literacy in History/Social Studies, Science, and Technical Subjects* (Council of Chief State School Officers & National Governors Association, 2010) includes a section on Foundational Skills (K–5) with specific attention to print concepts, phonological awareness, phonics, word recognition, and fluency. A detailed progression of skills and strategies related to what readers and writers should know and be able to do from the emergent stage through fifth grade is presented.

School districts have a responsibility to clarify to teachers what is expected of them and their students at various grade levels or grade-level groupings (e.g., primary) relative to the standards. Curriculum frameworks should be linked to the standards and include a delineation of the specific objectives involved with suggested strategies for instruction and ongoing assessment. Staff development is critical to ensuring that the curriculum frameworks are addressed in a manner that reflects a school district's philosophy and intent. This chapter offers a framework with concrete suggestions for linking standards, instruction, and assessment.

Curriculum Frameworks for Decoding Instruction (K–2)

Figures 16, 17, and 18 offer examples of curriculum frameworks for teaching word identification strategies, including phonics, in kindergarten and first and second grades. The idea is to give teachers clear guidance for instruction as well as ways to gather evidence about what children know and where they need help. Under the best circumstances, guidelines of this type would be developed cooperatively by teachers, administrators, and parents so that all involved would have a shared vision of what students should know and how they should perform at a particular level of instruction.

In addition, there would be some agreement on the kinds of instructional strategies that are used and the assessment strategies in place to document progress. Teachers would be expected to show evidence of planning for these to occur. Benchmarks outlining acceptable levels of performance also could be established. Note that in the examples given, the instructional strategies are similar for first and second grades. The key difference in these two grades is the use of increasingly difficult materials. Some differences will occur in the range of word recognition strategies covered at these two grade levels. (Please note that these curriculum frameworks are not meant to be prescriptive, but to serve as guides for districts to develop their own frameworks for use by classroom teachers.)

Figure 16. Kindergarten Curriculum Framework

Typical state standard for reading
Students apply a wide range of strategies to comprehend, interpret, evaluate, and appreciate texts.

Typical district grade-level application (decoding only)—Kindergarten level

Students have knowledge and use of the following:

    Directionality—left page before right, top to bottom, and left to right line of print and return sweep

    Visual matching—short sentences, phrases, words, and letters

(continued)

Figure 16. Kindergarten Curriculum Framework (continued)

Locating known words—letters in familiar text, high-frequency phrases and words

Alphabet knowledge—identify and match most uppercase and lowercase letters

Phonemic awareness—hear separate words in sentences and syllables in words, match like sounds in words (beginning and end), and recognize rhyming words

Phonics—alphabetic principle (awareness), knowledge of some initial consonant sound–letter relationships

Small sight vocabulary—recognizes own name, some high-frequency environmental print

Independent practice—makes use of opportunities to read and write independently

Instructional strategies

- Read aloud to children from a wide variety of materials.
- Involve children in a variety of shared reading and writing activities.
- Involve children in varied reader-response activities (e.g., art, drama, writing).
- Involve children in activities designed to help them use the conventions of written language: directionality, concept of a word, and the language of literacy.
- Involve children in activities designed to promote phonemic awareness, awareness of alphabetic principle, and some sound–letter correspondences.
- Involve children in activities designed to help them visually match sentences, words, letters (uppercase and lowercase), and other symbols.
- Involve children in activities designed to help them learn letter names.
- Provide time for independent reading.
- Make a wide variety of materials available.
- Provide opportunities for children to acquire a small sight vocabulary.
- Encourage children to engage in book activities outside the classroom.

Assessment strategies

- Documented observations during whole- and small-group instruction (e.g., anecdotal records, work samples).
- Assessment during one-to-one conferences (e.g., anecdotal records, developmental checklists, inventories).
- Monitoring system for at-home reading.
- Informal documentation of interest in books and attempts at independent reading.
- Documentation of independent writing (e.g., work samples).

Teachers are responsible for the following:

Evidence of regularly planned activities of the type listed under instructional strategies.

Current documentation for each child based on procedures listed under assessment strategies.

Figure 17. First-Grade Curriculum Framework

Typical state standard for reading
Students apply a wide range of strategies to comprehend, interpret, evaluate, and appreciate texts.

Typical district grade-level application (decoding only)—First grade (Also see kindergarten list)
Students demonstrate knowledge and use of the following:

Onset–rime analogies—use patterns in known words to identify unfamiliar words

Phonemic awareness—match similar medial sounds in short words, segment and blend phonemes in short words

Phonics—initial and final consonants, medial consonants, initial consonant clusters, initial and final consonant digraphs, and short and long vowels and some vowel generalizations

Structural analysis—compound words, some contractions, common inflectional endings

Multiple cueing systems for word recognition—semantics (word meaning), syntax (grammatical structure), and graphophonic (sounds–letters)

Cross-checking (one cue against another)

Self-correction strategies to preserve meaning

Sight vocabulary of high-frequency words and interesting words

Independent practice—make use of opportunities to read and write independently

Instructional strategies
Apply strategies at increasingly difficult levels:

- Read aloud to children from a wide variety of materials—narratives, expository, and poetry.
- Involve children in shared-reading activities.
- Involve children in varied reader-response activities, including writing.
- Involve children in activities designed to help them use graphophonic, semantic, and syntactic cues for reading.
- Involve children in activities designed specifically to promote the use of phonics in reading and spelling.
- Involve children in activities designed to help them segment language.
- Involve children in activities designed to help them use their background knowledge to make sense of what they are reading.
- Involve children in activities designed to help them learn to use the conventions of written language to make sense of what they are reading.
- Provide time for daily independent reading.
- Make a wide variety of materials available, including technology.

(continued)

Figure 17. First-Grade Curriculum Framework (continued)

- Involve children in high-frequency vocabulary activities connected to meaningful content.
- Involve children in rereading activities to develop fluency.
- Involve children in an ongoing home reading program.

Assessment

- Documented observations during whole- and small-group instruction (e.g., anecdotal records, work samples).
- Assessment during one-to-one conferences (e.g., running records, developmental checklists, inventories).
- Monitoring system for at-home reading.
- Documentation of independent reading (booklists).
- Documentation of independent writing (analysis of work samples).

Teachers are responsible for the following:

Evidence of regularly planned activities of the type listed under instructional strategies.

Current documentation for each child based on procedures listed under assessment strategies.

Figure 18. Second-Grade Curriculum Framework

Typical state standard for reading
Students apply a wide range of strategies to comprehend, interpret, evaluate, and appreciate texts.

Typical district grade level application (decoding only)—Second grade
(Also see first-grade list)
Students demonstrate knowledge and use of the following:

Multiple cueing systems for word recognition—semantics (word meaning), syntax (grammatical structure), and graphophonic (sounds–letters)

Cross-checking (one cue against another)

Self-correction strategies to preserve meaning

Phonemic awareness—increasing ability to segment words for phonics/spelling

Onset–rime analogies—increasing ability to use patterns in known words to identify unknown words

(continued)

Figure 18. Second-Grade Curriculum Framework (continued)

Phonics—increasing ability to use knowledge of short, long, and some vowel generalizations, consonant clusters and digraphs (initial and final; two and three letter), hard and soft g, and others to be determined by the teacher

Structural analysis—increasingly difficult root/base words, prefixes, suffixes, compound words, contractions, and common inflectional endings

Independent practice—make use of opportunities to read and write material of increasing difficulty independently

Sight vocabulary of high-frequency words is expanded

Instructional strategies

Apply strategies at increasingly difficult levels:

- Read aloud to children from a wide variety of materials—narratives, expository, and poetry.
- Involve children in shared-reading activities.
- Involve children in varied reader-response activities, including writing.
- Involve children in activities designed to help them use graphophonic, semantic, and syntactic cues for reading.
- Involve children in activities designed specifically to promote the use of phonics in reading and spelling.
- Involve children in activities designed to help them segment language.
- Involve children in activities designed to help them use their background knowledge to make sense of what they are reading.
- Involve children in activities designed to help them learn to use the conventions of written language to make sense of what they are reading.
- Provide time for daily independent reading.
- Make a wide variety of materials available, including technology.
- Involve children in a variety of vocabulary activities connected to meaningful content.
- Involve children in rereading activities to develop fluency.
- Involve children in an ongoing home reading program.

Assessment

- Documented observations during whole- and small-group instruction (e.g., anecdotal records, work samples).
- Assessment during one-to-one conferences (e.g., running records, developmental checklists, inventories).
- Monitoring system for at-home reading.
- Documentation of independent reading (e.g., list of books read).
- Documentation of independent writing (e.g., analysis of independent writing).

(continued)

> **Figure 18. Second-Grade Curriculum Framework (continued)**
>
> **Teachers are responsible for the following:**
>
> **Evidence of regularly planned activities of the type listed under instructional strategies.**
>
> **Current documentation for each child based on procedures listed under assessment strategies.**

Monitoring Progress

Shared and guided reading and writing most often are group experiences. As group activities, they lend themselves to an overall assessment of the students involved. However, group activities can also provide a window into the development of individuals. Because of behavior exhibited during a group activity, a student may be selected for special monitoring. For example, a child may rarely participate in the group. In this case, there is a need to determine whether this is due to low ability, shyness, health factors (such as vision or hearing problems), or other reasons. Or a child may appear to be functioning at a very advanced level, and closer observations can help determine whether this child is ready for more challenging materials.

Checklists offer a guide to the instructional components that might be addressed and monitored during instruction. Each school district is likely to construct its own set of guidelines, which should be made available for parents if they wish to examine them. Figure 19 is a detailed list of items usually included on checklists for emergent literacy and beginning reading programs. Keep in mind that the list focuses on strategies designed primarily to promote word recognition. It can be helpful for teachers who wish to construct their own checklists for the analysis of work samples and for assessment. Every district should have a literacy curriculum in place that goes beyond this list to include strategies specific to reading comprehension, literary analysis, and written composition at the beginning reading level. Checklists of the type shown in Figure 20 are typical of tools used for recording and assessing the observations of children's progress.

Figure 19. Assessing Young Children's Emerging Literacy Development

Observing children's literacy behavior on an informal basis is one of the best ways to determine how a child is progressing. The work of Marie Clay (1989) provides the basis for most checklists of emerging literacy. The checklists serve as an assessment for teachers as well. These skills and demonstrations of understanding cannot be observed unless we provide the environment for them to occur. *Keep in mind that the concepts related to emerging literacy are best learned through daily experiences with print and books and not through drill.*

Concepts about books and print

The child demonstrates an understanding and use of the following:

_____ Directionality of reading material:

_____ right side up _____ front to back

_____ left to right _____ top to bottom

_____ Title _____ Author _____ Illustrator

_____ Print as a source of meaning and language

_____ Pictures as sources of meaning

_____ Words/wordness: _____ as composed of letters _____ as matched to speech

_____ spaces between words

_____ Language to talk about literacy: word, letter, book, story, poem, page, line, title, author, illustrator, beginning, end, and so on.

Interest in books, reading, and writing

The child:

_____ shows an interest in listening to stories read aloud.

_____ participates in reading patterned and predictable language.

_____ engages in talk about books; recalls important parts and information in the stories.

_____ requests favorite books, such as nursery rhymes.

_____ chooses to look at books as an independent activity.

_____ views himself or herself as a reader.

_____ makes attempts at writing (in whatever way he or she can) and reads what was written.

_____ shows an awareness of the many purposes for reading and writing.

_____ shows an increasing curiosity about the world and a growing understanding and willingness to talk about new concepts and ideas.

Figure 20. Assessing Knowledge and Use of Word Recognition Strategies for Beginning Reading

Attention to components and patterns in the language: Foundational strategies

Note: These strategies usually are included in the kindergarten and early first-grade curriculum. They are taught through a balance of direct and indirect instruction. This list does not focus specifically on strategies for reading comprehension, literary analysis, or written composition.

The child:

_____ infers, orally, words in cloze-type activities (he or she fills in the acceptable word when the adult pauses during oral reading).

_____ matches, visually, repeated words and phrases.

_____ recognizes own name and its individual letters.

_____ recognizes increasing number of letters other than those in his or her own name.

_____ tracks print accurately with hand or finger.

_____ notices similarities in words and letters.

_____ recognizes when words rhyme.

_____ hears number of syllables.

_____ has small, but increasing and stable, sight vocabulary.

Attention to components and patterns in the language: Phonics and word analysis

Note: These generally are included in the first-grade curriculum over the course of an entire year.

The child demonstrates knowledge and use of the following:

_____ initial and final consonants

_____ short and long vowels

_____ initial consonant blends

_____ initial consonant digraphs

_____ some vowel generalizations (cvc, cvvc, cvc+e)

_____ onset–rime analogies

_____ compound words

_____ inflectional endings (-ing, -ed)

_____ plurals with s

_____ contractions

Observations During Oral Reading

The child:

_____ reads with appropriate expression.

_____ self-corrects to preserve meaning.

_____ observes punctuation to construct meaning.

(continued)

Figure 20. Assessing Knowledge and Use of Word Recognition Strategies for Beginning Reading (continued)

_____ takes risks in pronunciation of unfamiliar words when reading new materials.

_____ is strategic when confronting unfamiliar words.

For example,
- skips the word and continues to read for more information
- rereads the sentence
- uses context clues
- uses picture clues
- uses knowledge of familiar words and word parts (analogies)
- attempts to sound out the word

Observations During Writing

The child:

_____ applies phonics and word analysis strategies in attempting to spell.

_____ uses spaces between words.

_____ takes risks in attempting to spell.

_____ writes some words using conventional spelling.

_____ shows development in the use of capitalization:
uses _I_ at the beginning of sentences; capitalizes names of people and places.

_____ shows development in the use of punctuation.

Anecdotal records taken during and after group work or one-to-one conferences can provide direction for decision making about future learning experiences. Some teachers use a clipboard and labels to quickly write down their thoughts. These are later placed in the teacher's plan book or in a child's folder. Figure 21 shows some anecdotal notes written by a first-grade teacher who has made a special effort to track a child's behavior during group writing activities.

Work samples can provide insight into how well a group and the individuals within a group are progressing. When these are produced under the teacher's close direction, immediate feedback is given to problems associated with both teaching and learning. When similar problems occur across a large number of students, it signals the teacher to stop the lesson and revisit the material under study.

Work samples acquired through independent work are excellent sources of information, because they let the teacher know how well a child is able to apply known strategies to new situations. Samples of written material

Figure 21. First-Grade Teacher's Anecdotal Notes

9/15 Byron does not participate in shared writing but seems attentive.

9/29 B offered the *b* to begin the word *bird*—a start.

10/10 B seems to have caught on to what sound and symbols are all about.
Contributed several times during group writing.

Figure 22. First-Grade Work Sample

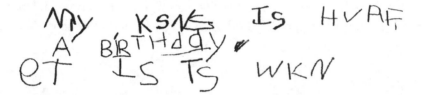

"My cousin is having a birthday. It is this weekend."

Teacher's comments: Kay is really attending to the sounds in words. She stretches the words and makes sure to include at least one letter to represent all the sounds she hears. She is beginning to use periods at the end of sentences. She used the word wall to help her spell the word birthday. She enjoys talking about her writing.

composed by the child and assessments of oral reading from new material on the child's instructional level offer the most useful information (see the first-grade work sample in Figure 22). Again, teachers try to determine how well a child is doing in relation to the group and in relation to himself or herself over time and try to identify the problems that seem to persist across the group that indicate a need for whole-group or small-group attention.

Monitoring At-Home and Independent Reading

A planned program for independent reading is indispensable. Time for reading self-selected books in school and a system for sharing books at home offers the child more time on task. It also involves the home in a way that makes it an active part of the process and offers an opportunity to monitor the child's development over time. Developing a simple but focused system for the use of materials at home lets everyone involved know how important an independent reading program is. The at-home reading buddy may be a parent, an older sibling, or any interested person who is willing to help. Figure 23 shows a Reading-At-Home form that can be duplicated and sent home along with the book. The Read-At-Home Log in Figure 24 can be completed at school by the child. A log such as this may be used for independent reading at school as well.

Teachers have an important influence on how much time children spend reading independently both during school and after school hours.

Figure 23. Reading-At-Home Form

TO: At-Home Reading Buddy

FROM: ___Mrs. Roades___

Please read the enclosed book with your reading buddy. Do at least one activity, fill out the form, and return it tomorrow. Thank you.

(Name of child) ___**Sammy Clayton**___ and I

read (Name of book) ___**Hop On Frog**___ together.

We also... (briefly tell what else you did) ___**We talked about the**___
___**Story and Sammy drew a picture of the frog.**___

Following are suggested activities that can be done with any book:

Discuss the story.	Read the story again with another reading buddy.
Draw a picture to go with the book.	Tape record a second reading at home.
Write another story like this one.	Make a puppet of one of the story characters.
Act out parts of the story.	Write about your favorite part.

___**Bill Clayton**___ Date ___**Jan. 24**___
(signed by Reading Buddy at home)

Figure 24. Read-At-Home Log

Book Title	Student's Name or Initials

Those who are successful in increasing home reading practice for their students have a deliberate plan in place and make it a high priority. They consistently supply appropriate books, have a system for monitoring home reading experiences, and encourage both children and their home partners to make reading a priority.

IDEA TO THINK AND TALK ABOUT

1. Examine your state's standards for beginning reading. Check to see which standards relate specifically to phonics and word study. Compare what you find with the continuum of expectations outlined here.

CHAPTER 7

Articulating the Phonics Program to Parents and the Community

I n my travels around the country, I have the good fortune to speak to parents, school board members, and educators. It will come as no surprise that there is great apprehension over the public perception that schools are not as good as they used to be—especially when it comes to teaching basic skills. Following are some of the questions that I am most frequently asked, followed by my responses in which I speak directly to the parent or caregiver. I hope that these prove useful as talking points for discussion.

Why Don't They Teach Phonics Anymore?

The teaching of phonics never has been abandoned. However, it is likely to look different today than it did when you were in school. Today's young children are just as likely to learn phonics through their writing as they are through their reading. Emphasis is placed on using phonics in conjunction with other word recognition strategies. Nevertheless, you may have good reason to question whether your child is receiving enough instruction in word recognition. Speak to your child's teacher and ask him or her to explain how phonics is addressed in the reading and writing program.

Is There a Certain Amount of Phonics That All Children Should Have?

No. The term *phonics* really refers to *instruction* in sound–letter relationships. Because some children figure out these relations with very little instruction, it is foolish to waste their time with something that is meant to help them do what they already know how to do. On the other hand, some children do need extensive help with phonics. In most classrooms, teachers provide a relatively standard curriculum for all students, which is modified to meet the varied needs of individuals. They do this by observing children's attempts as they read and spell. Based on these observations, teachers work with individuals and small groups to provide additional help.

How Will I Know Whether My Child Is Receiving Enough Phonics Instruction or When There Is a Reading Problem?

First, it is important to realize that you will be unable to tell how much phonics a child is receiving by the number of worksheets and workbook pages he or she brings home. Because today's teachers are more likely to teach phonics in a way that requires them to apply it directly to their reading and writing, rather than as an isolated exercise, children will receive instruction in conjunction with reading and writing of real texts, such as books, stories, and charts. Practice of these skills and strategies will involve more work with real texts rather than skill sheets.

You do have important windows through which you can observe your child's use of phonics, however. One is by observing your child's reading errors during oral reading. The other is by observing your child's spelling attempts during writing. You probably have some idea of what should be expected. Nevertheless, you might want to note the kinds of errors you observe and consult with your child's teacher as to whether these are things he or she should be expected to know.

Keep in mind that all mistakes are not equal. At times, when your child gives a word other than the one written on the page, you may want to ask "What made you say that?" You may find that the problem involves something other than phonics. Equally important, you may gain some insight as to how your child attempts to make sense of written material.

Should Phonics Instruction Continue Throughout the Grades?

Phonics instruction should be concentrated in the first few grades. Alternative strategies and special instructional programs may need to be provided for children who have had the benefit of a sound phonics program and who still are experiencing difficulty learning to read and write. Instruction in structural analysis, which often is confused with phonics, continues throughout the grades.

Is It Possible for a Child to Have Too Much Phonics?

Yes. Children who demonstrate the ability to apply phonics successfully in conjunction with other word recognition strategies should spend their time on challenging reading and writing activities, rather than the phonics activities designed for the whole class. Some children may have been taught phonics at the expense of other word recognition strategies, leaving them with an overreliance on one method of word recognition. These children are likely to become stuck, with no alternative word recognition strategies, when they see words for which phonics alone will not work. These children need a better balance of word identification strategies and need help with the ability to cross check and self-correct during the use of those strategies.

When Teachers Allow Children to Invent Spelling, Isn't That Teaching Incorrect Spelling?

No. Children are aware that their temporary spellings do not conform to adult standards. They understand that their attempts only approximate what is conventional, just as a baby's first steps and early speech only approximate adult behavior. Allowing children to apply what they know about phonics to help them spell is an important first step in helping them become independent writers, and it frees them to communicate their ideas. They realize that their spelling will change with increasing experience with written language and continued instruction.

At What Age Should Children Be Expected to Learn Correct Spelling?

As with all aspects of literacy, spelling is developmental. Children progress at different rates. Teachers track the spelling development of their students.

They observe which aspects of children's spelling adhere to standard forms and which do not, intervening with group and individual instruction when appropriate. Keep in mind that children will continue to experiment with new words and spelling patterns as they need them in their writing. For example, a teacher may be satisfied with the spelling of the word *wrinkle* as *rinkl*, realizing that neither the silent *w* in *wr* nor the final *le* is something that has been covered instructionally and that *wrinkle* is not a word this child would be expected to have in his or her visual memory. Yet it was obviously an important word for this child to include in his or her story. Teachers make a distinction between what a child should and should not be held accountable for.

Is There a Point When Invented Spelling Should Stop?

Again, if we assume that instruction is continuing throughout the grades and children are held accountable for what has been taught, then it follows naturally that a student's spelling should become less and less unconventional. By third grade or so, teachers begin to look at specific patterns of error within a child's spelling and address those needs more specifically. Most teachers agree that there seem to be some issues that need constant revisiting, such as the homophones *there* and *their*. Some spelling generalizations and some aspects of word study such as Latin and Greek roots generally are not addressed during the primary grades.

What Should I Look for in My School's Beginning Literacy Program?

Even within the same district, schools can differ widely in their approach to literacy. Within the same school, teachers may vary in their overall approach even when they use the same materials. Nevertheless, you can get a sense of the overall stance or vision of a school by asking the teacher and principal a few questions in a direct, nonthreatening manner. Remember, even when the answers are not what you expected, you might want to take a wait-and-see approach and then express your concerns. More than likely you will want to ask questions and observe in classrooms to determine some of the following:

- *The school's general orientation toward literacy instruction*—Administrators and teachers should be able to explain, in simple terms, how they approach literacy instruction in general as well as how they address phonics. Beware if they merely say they use the XYZ program. Although you might want to see those materials, they should really be a reflection of the district's and teacher's philosophical stance and curriculum goals. Materials alone should not drive the curriculum. If you are especially worried about phonics and spelling, ask for one or two specific examples of how it is taught and how your child's progress will be monitored.

- *The curriculum goals for the grade level(s) you are most interested in*—Teachers should be able to give you a clear idea of what generally is expected of most children by the end of the year in the particular grade they teach. This may be included in a curriculum guide or in a parent booklet, teachers may orally share some general information about grade-level curriculum goals.

- *Library media facilities and access to technology*—Young children need plenty of opportunities and encouragement to practice the skills they are learning. Access to an abundance of interesting materials makes this practice possible. It is no wonder that virtually everyone agrees that a school's library collection is the backbone of literacy instruction. You should inquire about the classroom library and school library facilities as well as access to computers and other technology. You also will want to know if a professional library media specialist is available to work with teachers and students and how much access children have to books and other media on a daily basis.

- *Evidence of differentiated instruction*—Differentiating instruction to meet individual needs is perhaps the most important and challenging thing that teachers do. Is there evidence that the teacher varies instruction to include whole-group, small-group, and some personalized activities? Teachers who do this are more likely to get to know your child well and adapt instruction accordingly.

- *Provisions for children who are experiencing difficulty*—Although it is good to know that there are support programs outside the regular classroom, it is equally important to know how the classroom teacher addresses the problems of the struggling students. Among the things

Teacher and parent meet to discuss the child's progress in reading.

you might expect are extra small-group instruction, extra one-to-one conferences, and the use of special materials.

- *Provisions for children who are advanced in their literacy development*—More than likely, any special provisions for the advanced beginning readers will be concentrated in the classroom. You will want to know about plans to provide more challenging tasks and materials for these children.

- *The classroom procedures for monitoring progress*—There should be evidence of some type of ongoing classroom assessment. You might expect the teacher to keep folders with work samples, such as children's independent writing. Records of notes or checklists completed during one-to-one conferences also may be included as well as lists of books children have read independently. Beware if you simply are shown a report card rather than the evidence on which the report card grades are based, and be concerned if the folders are filled with skill sheets and workbook pages rather than applications of skills in meaningful situations.

• *The support for home and school connections*—Ask about what the school expects from parents and caregivers in the home. What types of homework activities are expected? Is homework based on a particular number of minutes per night, or is there an attempt to provide meaningful home activities that are linked to the school curriculum? Is there a procedure for monitoring homework? Are parent meetings and conferences scheduled that might help you get a sense of the school program?

What Can I Do at Home to Help My Child Read and Write?

Obviously, the activities you might do at home to encourage reading and writing are similar to those listed in Chapter 5. Nevertheless, I will emphasize some that are particularly important as support from the home.

• Every topic listed in Chapter 5 is best developed at home in an informal, risk-free environment. Print awareness, print concepts, the functions of print, a knowledge of narrative structure, and literacy as a source of enjoyment are the foundation on which phonemic awareness and phonics are built.

• Read to and with your child on a daily basis. When reading familiar books, encourage your child to read along. Pause occasionally and let your child fill in an obvious word. Talk about the content of books and relate the content to your shared experience and to other books.

• Read and reread favorite nursery rhymes. Sing favorite songs and rhymes, reinforcing the language patterns and rhyme.

• Balance exposure to print books with other media, such as computer technology. Use the same care in selecting computer games and activities as you do when selecting books.

• When your child begins to read independently, show him or her how proud you are of each new accomplishment.

• When your child comes to an unfamiliar word, wait before you interject an answer. He or she may be attempting to figure it out independently. After a while, you might ask what he or she thinks might make sense or how the word might sound.

- If your child is making a great number of errors, the book probably is too hard. Ask the teacher to suggest easier material. If this is "required reading," read the book to the child first and then ask him or her to read it to you. Meanwhile, continue to read easier material to build confidence and allow your child to practice skills.

- Write with your child. Allow him or her to help with the spelling of words for grocery lists or family reminders to be posted on the refrigerator. Offer praise for his or her help with the parts of words he or she knows.

- Play simple word games: "I am thinking of a word..."

  It rhymes with *play*. (*day, say*)

  It tastes good on toast and it begins like *ball*. (*butter*)

  Accept any reasonable answer. After the child catches on, have him or her make up a riddle for you to answer.

- When your child attempts to write independently, first pay attention to the content—what he or she is trying to say. Then, praise him or her for the parts of words spelled correctly as well as those completely correct by conventional standards. Also praise any attempts that suggest progress beyond what has been introduced at school or that you would not expect him or her to know. You might make a comment about sound–letter relationships you think he or she should know and offer a reminder or help. If he or she wishes to revise or edit his or her work, you can offer to help. Remember, it is important that children understand that you do not expect every word to be spelled conventionally. You are looking for overall progress toward conventional spelling, however.

Today's educators are acutely aware of the importance of good public relations, both with parents and with the broader community at large. A truly effective home–school communication program is one that anticipates the kinds of concerns that parents may have and launches a strong proactive effort to enlist parental and community support before major misunderstandings develop. In many cases, the questions and concerns parents raise are those they should not have to ask in the first place. Potentially misunderstood aspects of the curriculum should be well articulated through ongoing efforts such as parent conferences, workshops, and newsletters. Educators need the insight and energy of the most concerned parents as allies, not opponents. Both share the same goal— the best education for children.

IDEA TO THINK AND TALK ABOUT

1. Discuss how you might use the ideas in this chapter to plan a series of activities to promote better understanding of and involvement by parents in an early literacy program.

Phonics Quiz for Teachers

Throughout this book, many phonics-related terms have been used. You may have only a vague recollection of them from your early years as a student learning to read. As a skilled reader yourself, you may wonder how you learned to read without knowing all these terms. The truth is that you can be a highly accomplished reader without knowing very much *about* phonics. As you learned to read, you focused on the *use* of phonics and other word recognition strategies.

Now as someone who has chosen to assist others in learning to read, you are taking time to step outside the reading process and think of it as an object to be analyzed and discussed. This requires knowing something about the various strategies that typically are taught as well as the labels for them. Knowledge about phonics will help you to evaluate and use instructional materials and curriculum guides. The following quiz is excerpted partly from *Phonics Test for Teachers* (Durkin, 1964). You might like to try it with a friend. Discuss the reasons for your answers before you check the answer key on pages 90–91. *Remember, this is not offered as something to be used with children. It is offered as background information for those who wish to help children learn to read.*

Phonics Quiz for Teachers

Vowels: Long and Short
Very often, vowels record what are generally called "long" sounds and "short" sounds. Knowledge of both sounds, for each of the five vowels, is evaluated here.

A. In each of the five rows of words listed below, underline the *one* word that begins with a *long* vowel sound.

1. all	ask	apron
2. eager	early	edge
3. ignore	idle	irrigate
4. odd	ocean	order
5. up	urge	use

B. In each of the five rows of words listed below, underline the *one* word that begins
with a *short* vowel sound.

1.	ace	all	at
2.	eagle	earn	engine
3.	ice	ill	irk
4.	octave	owl	over
5.	ugly	use	urgent

Vowel Generalizations

Certain factors within a word affect the sounds recorded by the vowels in that word.
Knowledge of these factors is evaluated below.

Answer each section by checking the appropriate blank and by writing the relevant
generalization.

A.   a i f
  1. If *aif* were a syllable in a word, the
     letter *a* in that syllable would probably:

                              _____ sound like the *a* in *ate*
                              _____ sound like the *a* in *ask*
                              _____ be silent

  2. The letter *i* in that syllable would probably:

                              _____ sound like the *i* in *ice*
                              _____ sound like the *i* in *inch*
                              _____ be silent

  3. Why would *a* and *i* most likely record these sounds?

B.   e k
  1. If *ek* were a syllable in a word, the
     letter *e* in that syllable would probably:

                              _____ sound like the *e* in *eat*
                              _____ sound like the *e* in *end*
                              _____ be silent

  2. Why would the letter *e* most likely record this sound?

C.   b u
  1. If *bu* were a syllable in a word, the
     letter *u* in that syllable would probably:

                              _____ sound like the *u* in *use*
                              _____ sound like the *u* in *us*
                              _____ be silent

  2. Why would *us* most likely record this sound?

(continued)

Digraphs

Certain combinations of consonants are called *digraphs*. Knowledge of the consonant digraphs and of the digraph sounds is evaluated here.

A. Define the term *consonant digraph*:

B. In the words listed randomly below, find the eight words that contain a consonant digraph. In each of these eight words, underline the two letters that make up the digraph.

thief	stain	enough	dumb
chalet	phase	fish	write
crust	skip	try	there
sting	plane	rich	brown

Consonant Blends

Certain combinations of consonants are called *consonant blends*. Knowledge of consonant blends is evaluated here.

A. Define the term *consonant blend*:

B. Find the eight words that contain a consonant blend. In each of these eight words, underline the letters that make up the blend.

blank	comb	shout	trap
kite	spring	twig	camel
grain	gasp	foam	gnaw
split	write	cane	rusty

Diphthongs

Certain combinations of vowels are called *diphthongs*. At times, the consonants *y* and *w* function as vowels; consequently some diphthongs are a combination of a vowel with *y*, or a combination of a vowel with *w*. Knowledge of diphthongs is evaluated here.

A. Define the term *diphthong*:

B. In the words listed randomly below, find the six words that contain a diphthong. In each of these six words, underline the two letters that make up the diphthong.

oil	float	built
see	owl	few
bowl	they	couch
boy	pour	each

Answer Key

Vowels: Long and Short

A. Long vowel sounds | | | Long
	1. all	ask	***apron***	(a)
	2. ***eager***	early	edge	(e)
	3. ignore	***idle***	irrigate	(i)
	4. odd	***ocean***	order	(o)
	5. up	urge	***use***	(u)

B. Short vowel sounds | | | Short
	1. ace	all	***at***	(a)
	2. eagle	earn	***engine***	(e)
	3. ice	***ill***	irk	(i)
	4. ***octave***	owl	over	(o)
	5. ***ugly***	use	urgent	(u)

Vowel Generalizations

A. If *aif* were a syllable in a word:

1. The *a* would probably sound like the *a* in *ate*.
2. The *i* would be silent.
3. When there are two vowels (in this case, *a* and *i*) in a syllable, the first is usually long and the second is silent, as in *aid* and *note*.

B. If *ek* were a syllable in a word:

1. The *e* would probably sound like the *e* in *end*.
2. When there is one vowel (here, *e*) followed by a consonant in the same syllable, that vowel is usually short, as in *at* and *up*.

C. If *bu* were a syllable in a word:

1. The *u* would probably sound like the *u* in *use*.
2. When there is one vowel (here, *u*) in a syllable, but it is at the end of the syllable, it is usually long, as in *be* and *clover*.

Digraphs

A. A consonant digraph is a combination of two consonants representing a sound unlike that of either of the individual consonants.

B.

1	thief	stain	2	enough	dumb
3	chalet	4 phase	5	fish	write
	crust	skip		try	6 there
7	sting	plane	8	rich	brown

Excerpted by permission of the publisher from Durkin, D., *Phonics Test for Teachers*, New York: Teachers College Press, © 1964 by Teachers College, Columbia University. All rights reserved. (continued)

Consonant Blends

A. A consonant blend is a combination of two or more consonants that are pronounced or blended together with minimal change in their sounds.

B.
1 <u>bl</u>ank	comb	shout	2 <u>tr</u>ap
kite	3 <u>spr</u>ing	4 <u>tw</u>ig	camel
5 <u>gr</u>ain	6 <u>g</u>as<u>p</u>	foam	gnaw
7 <u>spl</u>it	write	cane	8 ru<u>st</u>y

Diphthongs

A. A diphthong is a combination of two vowels recording a sound unlike that of either vowel. (Here, *y* and *w* function as vowels.)*

*Technically, too, a diphthong is a kind of sound which, in the process of being made, requires a change in the mouth position. It is for this reason that vowel combinations like *au* (*auto*) and *oo* (*look*) are not diphthongs.

Also to be remembered is that a diphthong is a particular sound, not just a particular combination of letters. This is why *ou* is considered a diphthong in *couch* but not in *four*.

B. Before checking your answers, write the diphthongs (underlined in the words below) in the parentheses before the numbers in the Summary space of the test booklet. List the diphthongs in the order in which they are numbered here. Then check the appropriate Right or Wrong blank for each diphthong.

1 <u>oi</u>l	float	built
see	2 <u>ow</u>l	3 f<u>ew</u>
bowl	4 the<u>y</u>	5 c<u>ou</u>ch
6 bo<u>y</u>	pour	each

Excerpted by permission of the publisher from Durkin, D., *Phonics Test for Teachers*, New York: Teachers College Press, © 1964 by Teachers College, Columbia University. All rights reserved.

REFERENCES

Adams, M.J. (1990). *Beginning to read: Thinking and learning about print.* Cambridge, MA: Harvard University Press.

Bear, D.R., Invernizzi, M., Templeton, S., & Johnston, F. (1996). *Words their way: Word study for phonics, vocabulary, and spelling instruction.* Upper Saddle River, NJ: Prentice Hall.

Berliner, D.C., & Biddle, B.J. (1995). *The manufactured crisis: Myths, fraud, and the attack on America's public schools.* Reading, MA: Addison-Wesley.

Bond, G., & Dykstra, R. (1967/1997). The cooperative research program in first-grade reading instruction. *Reading Research Quarterly, 32*(4), 348–427.

Castiglioni-Spalten, M.L., & Ehri, L.C. (2003). Phonemic awareness instruction: Contribution of articulatory segmentation to novice beginners' reading and spelling. *Scientific Studies of Reading, 7*(1), 25–52.

Castles, A., & Coltheart, M. (2004). Is there a causal link from phonological awareness to success in learning to read?, *91*(1), 77–111.

Chall, J.S. (1967). *Learning to read: The great debate.* New York: McGraw-Hill.

Chall, J.S. (1983). *Learning to read: The great debate* (Updated ed.). New York: McGraw-Hill.

Clay, M.M. (1989). *The early detection of reading difficulties* (3rd ed.). Portsmouth, NH: Heinemann.

Clymer, T. (1996). The utility of phonic generalization in the primary grades. *The Reading Teacher, 50*(3), 182–187.

Council of Chief State School Officers & National Governors Association (2010). *Common Core State Standards for English Language Arts & Literacy in History/Social Studies, Science, and Technical Subjects.* Retrieved October 7, 2010, from www.corestandards .org/assets/CCSSI_ELA%20Standards.pdf

Cunningham, P.M., & Cunningham, J.W. (1992). Making words: Enhancing the invented spelling-decoding connection. *The Reading Teacher, 46*(2), 106–115.

Durkin, D. (1964). *Phonics test for teachers.* New York: Teachers College Press.

Ehri, L.C., & Roberts, T. (2006). The roots of learning to read and write: Acquisition of letters and phonemic awareness. In D.K. Dickinson & S.B. Neuman (Eds.), *Handbook of early literacy research* (Vol. 2, pp. 113–131). New York: Guilford.

Flesch, R. (1955). *Why Johnny can't read: And what you can do about it.* New York: Harper.

Fox, B.J. (1996). *Strategies for word identification: Phonics from a new perspective.* Englewood Cliffs, NJ: Merrill.

Galda, L., Cullinan, B.E., & Strickland, D.S. (1997). *Language, literacy, and the child* (2nd ed.). Orlando, FL: Harcourt Brace.

Ganske, K. (2000). *Word journeys: Assessment-guided phonics, spelling, and vocabulary instruction.* New York: Guilford.

Gaskins, I.W., Ehri, L.C., Cress, C., O'Hara, C., & Donnelly, K. (1996). Procedures for word learning: Making discoveries about words. *The Reading Teacher, 50*(4), 312–327.

Goswami, U. (2001). Early phonological development and the acquisition of literacy. In S.B. Neuman & D.K. Dickinson (Eds.), *Handbook of early literacy research* (Vol. 1, pp. 111–125). New York: Guilford.

Heilman, A. (1989). *Phonics in proper perspective* (6th ed.). Englewood Cliffs, NJ: Merrill/ Prentice Hall.

Hintze, J.M., Ryan, A.L., & Stoner, G. (2003). Concurrent validity and diagnostic accuracy of the Dynamic Indicators of Basic Early Literacy Skills and the Comprehensive Test of Phonological Processing. *School Psychology Review, 32*(4), 541–556.

Kibby, M. (1993). What reading teachers should know about reading proficiency in the U.S. *Journal of Reading, 37*(1), 28–40.

Korkeamaki, R.-L., & Dreher, M.J. (1993). Finland, phonics, and whole language: Beginning reading in a regular letter-sound correspondence language. *Language Arts, 70*(6), 475–482.

Krashen, S.D. (1993). *The power of reading: Insights from the research.* Englewood, CO: Libraries Unlimited.

Labbo, L.D. (2006). Five internet sites too good to miss. *The Reading Teacher, 59*(8), 810–812.

Labbo, L.D., & Kuhn, M. R. (2000). Weaving chains of affect and cognition: A young child's understanding of CD-ROM talking books. *Journal of Literacy Research, 32*(2), 187–210.

Leslie, L., & Caldwell, J. (1995). *Qualitative Reading Inventory-II.* New York: Harper Collins.

Manyak, P.C., & Bauer, E.B. (2008). Explicit code and comprehension instruction for English learners. *The Reading Teacher, 61*(5), 432–434.

Moustafa, M. (1995). Children's productive phonological recoding. *Reading Research Quarterly, 30*(3), 464–476.

Moustafa, M. (1997). Reconceptualizing phonics instruction. In C. Weaver (Ed.), *Reconsidering a balanced approach to reading* (pp. 135–157). Urbana, IL: National Council of Teachers of English.

National Commission on Excellence in Education. (1983). *A nation at risk: The imperative for educational reform.* Washington, DC: U.S. Department of Education.

National Institute for Literacy (2008). *Developing early literacy: Report of the National Early Literacy Panel.* Washington, DC: Author.

National Institute of Child Health and Human Development. (2000). *Report of the National Reading Panel. Teaching children to read: An evidence-based assessment of the scientific research literature on reading and its implications for reading instruction* (NIH Publication No. 00-4769). Washington, DC: U.S. Government Printing Office.

Powell, D., & Hornsby, D. (1993). *Learning phonics and spelling in a whole language classroom.* New York: Scholastic.

Read, C. (1971). Pre-school children's knowledge of English phonology. *Harvard Educational Review, 41*(1), 1–34.

Read, C. (1975). *Children's categorization of speech sounds in English* (Rep. No. 17). Urbana, IL: National Council of Teachers of English Committee on Research.

Rutherford, W. (1968). Learning to read: A critique. *The Elementary School Journal, 69*(2), 72–83.

Salinger, T. (2006). Policy decisions in early literacy assessment. In D.K. Dickinson & S.B. Neuman (Eds.), *Handbook of early literacy research* (Vol. 2, pp. 427–444). New York: Guilford.

Shanahan, T., & Beck, I.L. (2006). Effective literacy teaching for English-language learners. In D. August & T. Shanahan (Eds.), *Developing literacy in second-language learners: Report of the National Literacy Panel on language-minority children and youth* (pp. 415–488). Mahwah, NJ: Erlbaum.

Strickland, D.S. (2004, Winter). Literacy in early childhood education: The search for balance. *Children and Families, 18*(1), 24–31.

Strickland, D.S., Ganske, K., & Monroe, J.K. (2002). *Supporting struggling readers and writers: Strategies for classroom intervention, 3-6.* Portland, ME: Stenhouse; Newark, DE: International Reading Association.

Strickland, D.S., & Shanahan, T. (2004). Laying the groundwork for literacy. *Educational Leadership, 61*(6), 74–77.

Teale, W.H., & Yokota, J. (2000). Beginning reading and writing: Perspectives on instruction. In D.S. Strickland & L.M. Morrow (Eds.), *Beginning reading and writing* (pp. 3–21). New York: Teachers College Press.

Treiman, R. (1985). Onsets and rimes as units of spoken syllables: Evidence from children. *Journal of Experimental Child Psychology, 39*(1), 161–181.

Vähäpassi, A. (1977a). *On the structure and variability of reading skill in grade 3 of the comprehensive school in school year 1973–1974* (Rep. No. 283). Jyväskylä, Finland: University of Jyväskylä, Institute for Educational Research.

Vähäpassi, A. (1977b). *The level of reading and writing in grade 6 of the comprehensive school in school year 1974–1975* (Rep. No. 88). Jyväskylä, Finland: University of Jyväskylä, Institute for Educational Research.

Vähäpassi, A. (1987). *The level of reading comprehension in the Finnish comprehensive school: Publication series A* (Res. Rep. No. 10). Jyväskylä, Finland: University of Jyväskylä, Institute for Educational Research.

Venezky, R.L. (1973). Letter-sound generalizations of first-, second-, and third-grade Finnish children. *Journal of Educational Psychology, 64*(3), 288–292.

Wasburn-Moses, L. (2006). 25 best Internet sources for teaching reading. *The Reading Teacher, 60*(1), 70–75.

Weaver, C. (1994). *Reading process and practice* (2nd ed.). Portsmouth, NH: Heinemann.

Weaver, C. (1998). Experimental research: On phonemic awareness and on whole language. In C. Weaver (Ed.), *Reconsidering a balanced approach to reading* (pp. 321–371). Urbana, IL: National Council of Teachers of English.

Wylie, R.E., & Durrell, D.D. (1970). Teaching vowels through phonograms. *Elementary English, 47*(6), 787–791.

Yopp, H.K. (1992). Developing phonemic awareness in young children. *The Reading Teacher, 45*(9), 696–703.

Yopp, H.K., & Stapleton, L. (2008). Conciencia fonémica en Español (Phonemic awareness in Spanish). *The Reading Teacher, 61*(5), 374–382.

INDEX

Note. Page numbers followed by *f* and *t* indicate figures and tables, respectively.

Leslie, L., 44

letter recognition, 36

library media facilities, 82

literacy: definition of, 4; as source of enjoyment, 52

literacy instruction: communication with parents and community about, 81–84; description of, 4; early, goal of, 1; informal classroom assessment in, 41–45, 43*f*, 83; integration of language arts in, 29–32, 33*f*; materials for, 32, 33–41; trends in, 26; writing in, 26–29

literature-based curricula, 46–47

M

Mann, Horace, 6

Manyak, P.C., 62

materials for literacy instruction: basal or core reading programs, 6–7, –10, 34–37, 36*f*; multimedia technologies, 40–41; patterned texts, 37–39; trade books, 33–34; variety in, 32

Miss Bindergarten Gets Ready for Kindergarten, 52

modeling, 37–38, 56

monitoring: at-home and independent reading, 75–77, 76*f*, 77*f*; progress, 71–75*f*, 73–74*f*

Monroe, J.K., 63

morphemes, 18

morphemic knowledge, 17–18

Moustafa, M., 15, 16

multimedia technologies, 40–41

N

narrative structure, knowledge of, 51–52

A Nation at Risk: The Imperative for Educational Reform, 10

National Commission on Excellence in Education, 10

National Institute for Literacy, 8

National Institute of Child Health and Human Development, 8

National Reading Panel report, 8

novice spellers, 20*f*

word identification: curriculum frameworks for, 66–71*f*; instruction for, 4; strategies for reading, 12–16, 13*f*

word making activities, 57

word recognition checklist, 71, 72*f*, 73–74*f*

work samples, 44, 74–75, 75*f*

worksheets, assessment based on, 42, 43*f*

writing: copying and, 27–28, 27*f*; encouraging attempts at, 56–57; at home, 84–85; instruction in, in elementary years, 26–29; spelling and, 16–21; strategies for developing foundations of, 51–53

Writing/Phonics and Spelling Assessment Record (Pre K–3), 22, 23*f*

Wylie, R.E., 58

Y

Yokota, J., 26

Yopp, H.K., 4, 61

IRA publications are ideal for use in school-based professional learning communities and teacher education. Our books, journals, and online resources are designed to support professional growth for educators, from preservice teachers through literacy leaders. You'll find a range of adaptable and inexpensive resources, including study guides, video–book packages, podcasts, research-based lesson plans, and much more. For more information about making IRA part of your professional development, visit www.reading.org.